# A Cure for
# SLAVERY

*Problems and Fixes: Observations from the Bottom of the Pyramid and a Model for a New Economic System with a Nonprofit Central Bank*

WOODROW PARKER

Copyright © 2017 Woodrow Parker
All rights reserved
First Edition

PAGE PUBLISHING, INC.
New York, NY

First originally published by Page Publishing, Inc. 2017

ISBN 978-1-64138-464-3 (Paperback)
ISBN 978-1-64138-465-0 (Digital)

Printed in the United States of America

For my daughter and son

# Contents

Observations from the Bottom of the Pyramid ........................ 9
    Why I Decided to Write This Book ............................... 9
    Introduction ........................................................... 11
    Banks, the Source of Money ...................................... 12
    Crossroads .............................................................. 15
    Why Should I Support a Nonprofit Central Bank? ......... 16

Part I: Problems
    Chapter 1:  Banks ................................................. 23
        Money ................................................................ 28
        Interest ............................................................... 34
    Chapter 2:  Labor ................................................. 37
    Chapter 3:  Economy ............................................ 41
        Credit ................................................................ 47
        Fresh Money ....................................................... 50
        Debt .................................................................. 52
        Bubbles .............................................................. 55
    Chapter 4:  Profit ................................................. 60
        Microprofit ......................................................... 60
        Macroprofit ........................................................ 61

Chapter 5:   Wages ................................................................63
    Disposable Wages ...............................................63
    Income ..................................................................64
    Disposable Income ..............................................64

Chapter 6:   Cost of Living ....................................................65

Chapter 7:   Manufacturing ...................................................66

Chapter 8:   Pricing ...............................................................68
    Pricing Is the Throttle of the Economy ..............68
    Do High Prices Serve the Economy? ..................69
    How Much Is Enough? ........................................70
    Price Fixing ...........................................................71

Chapter 9:   Business .............................................................72

Chapter 10: Loans .................................................................75

Chapter 11: Government ......................................................77

Chapter 12: Health Care .......................................................79

Chapter 13: Education ..........................................................83

Chapter 14: War ....................................................................85

Chapter 15: Housing .............................................................86
    Valuation ................................................................87

Chapter 16: The Justice System ............................................90

Chapter 17: Taxes ..................................................................95

Chapter 18: Revolutions .......................................................97

Conclusion ................................................................................100

## Part II: Fixes

Model for a New Economic System with a Nonprofit
Central Bank (NPCB) ..............................................................107

Labor: As Good As Gold ..........................................................109

| | |
|---|---|
| There Is So Much Work to Do! | 112 |
| Earnings: Creating Money from Labor | 113 |
|     Earnings Bond | 115 |
|     Service Is Labor | 117 |
|     The New Consumer Class | 120 |
| Unlimited Potential | 122 |
| Design | 123 |
|     The Private Sector | 123 |
|     The NPCB Public Sector | 126 |
|     The NPCB Public Sector: Manufacturing | 128 |
|     The NPCB Public Sector: Labor | 128 |
|     The NPCB Public Sector: Education / Public Service Bonus | 129 |
|     The NPCB Public Sector: Health Care | 131 |
|     The Government Sector and the NPCB | 131 |
| Revelations | 133 |
|     Imagining the Possibilities | 133 |
|     Other Benefits | 135 |
|     Alternative Limits | 136 |
| Projected Impact Review | 138 |
|     Crime | 138 |
|     Families | 139 |
|     Justice | 140 |
|     Poverty | 141 |
|     Immigration | 142 |
|     Prostitution and Pornography | 142 |
|     New Industrial Sectors | 142 |

| | |
|---|---|
| Free and Fair Marketplace | 143 |
| Starvation | 143 |
| War | 144 |
| Appendix | 147 |
| Global Nonprofit Bank Guidelines | 147 |
| Private Sector | 147 |
| Public Sector | 149 |
| Basic Allowance | 151 |
| The Consumer Class | 151 |
| Bibliography | 159 |

# Observations from the Bottom of the Pyramid

## Why I Decided to Write This Book

I have always found it impossible to look at poverty, injustice, crime, and pollution without feeling a deep and overwhelming urge to cure these ills. I meditated on this and realized I needed more information. I needed to understand what the source of these malignancies are. I needed to understand what conditions existed to make people hurt themselves, others, and the beautiful world we live on. I started my education with philosophy, military science, and I let go of ideas that did not provide answers.

The problems with financial policies, regulations, and deregulations were plainly obvious, and somehow not one person in was willing to voice a cure. When pressed, the authorities returned to the flawed and benign economic/financial system time and again to justify blatant fraud and theft. "That's the system. It is the only one we have. There is no other way. It is not illegal." They shrugged.

I knew I could create a better system than the one that is responsible for the chaos and uncertainty, poverty, crime, war, and starvation currently plaguing 99 percent of the world and benefitting only the 1 percent. Its not rocket science! It is a collection of policies and guidelines that permit harmful behavior and encourage others to join in. To change the system is to change the policies and guidelines. I know humans are basically peaceful and have love in their hearts for one another in spite of the separations forced on humanity by economic status, religion, and ethnicity.

After a while, the universe started dropping nuggets of what I considered valuable information in my lap. I read these nuggets and listened to my gut and intuition. More and more, the fog cleared, and I could see how singular aspects of humanity, society, and the world fit together. They came into focus like a large jigsaw puzzle picture for the first time. I grew to understand what the puzzle was made out of. It was made out of a system of debt. So I sought to educate myself on the nature of money, how it works, where it comes from, and what it is used for. I came to the realization that the prevailing economic principal is all make-believe, and recently my opinion was validated by an article written by an economist that claimed all of modern economic theory is based on fallacy and this fallacious economic principal is the basis for political decision-making (1). That was the last piece. Suddenly, this crazy idea I had been trying to disprove became a potent answer to my questions and probably the solution to the majority of the world's woes.

I told people about my ideas for ten years, and they could not grasp it, having been programmed by decades of flawed economic principals exalted as financial gospel. I felt like I was Columbus trying to convince people the world was round. They were deaf to reason, but I know this is the best solution. I see fragments of the solution floating around the Internet, and perhaps now the mass consciousness will be open to these evolutionary concepts.

So I resolved to write this book and lay bare the problems and the solutions for all to see through my eyes. We human beings created these problems, so it is us that must be allowed to fix the problems and repair the damage that has been done. Even if it takes a hundred years for these ideas to penetrate the cognitive dissonance of humanity, it is worth it. It is the life raft of humanity, the best thing for all of us and the world.

# Introduction

My whole life I have struggled with money. Never having it in abundance, my family's life was dominated by the quest to seek it out in order to pay the rent, make dinner, have the power turned on, put gas in the car, or buy food.

Throughout my childhood, my family was poor. We were occasionally on welfare, played the food stamp game now and again, and always struggled to pay bills. It seemed just as we got enough, the bills went up and suddenly there wasn't enough anymore. We never made enough to save, and if we did somehow manage to have a little extra money, we spent it on some entertainment to be "normal" for a little while. Many nights our dinner choices were lima beans or lima beans.

I was ridiculed in adolescence because my clothes were tattered or unfashionable. I felt shame and feelings of inadequacy as a young adult because my family never had as much money as our neighbors. I was never able to do the things my friends did unless they paid my way. Most of the time, I refused to go, so as not to considered myself a mooch; often they insisted. Sometimes, when I was lonely or feeling like life was washing past me, I would go without protest. I thought of myself as a mooch anyway, but even mooches are entitled to some happiness.

When I reached teens, the inferior feelings engrained from childhood poverty struck my self-esteem so badly that I would never dare to ask a girl out on a date. I simply could not produce the money required for a dinner and a movie, and I felt ashamed. My parents didn't have it, so I didn't have it. I was too young to legally have a job.

When I was twelve or thirteen, I tried selling the candles I made door to door in my neighborhood without success. My discouragement led me into a psychological corner for the outcast and deficient. It felt unfair. I was a good person. I never stole anything of value, vandalized anything beautiful, acted out negatively, or deliberately lied to cause hurt or harm as some of my well-to-do peers did. I was smart and good-looking although I would never admit it to myself; I still saw myself as deficient.

The only thing I was deficient in was money. I felt powerless to change because most of my classmates got their money from their parents. None of them had jobs. A few had to earn their allowance by doing chores, but that's only when your parents have enough extra money to give you an allowance. I never had the money to express myself in the way we were all taught by the TV as the way to express your feelings to a lady. I could never win with the truth.

"I really wanted to bring you something nice, but I didn't have the money to buy it."

"I would really love to take you to this show and buy you a memento of our time together, but I don't have the money."

"I really think you're smart and funny and pretty, and I would love to get to know you better. Want to buy me some coffee?"

"Let's get married! Can you pay, okay?"

"So I made you this flower out of tissue paper, but what I really wanted to give you was a huge floral bouquet, because that's how pretty you are."

Most of the time, I just kept my head down and my mouth shut.

I have no special education in economics other than public school and a real estate license. My observations are made purely from my own experience trying to scratch a living from a broken and irrational financial system and witnessing failure after failure of business and the economy in my years of life.

This is the stage from which I observe the financial world—the bottom of the financial pyramid looking up today and beyond tomorrow.

## Banks, the Source of Money

### Tale of 100 Knights

Imagine the entire world, your country, your state, even your town as one realm where one hundred knights deposited one hundred pieces of gold in the vault of a noble's castle for safekeeping. As he was noble and presumably true to his word, they trusted him to be honest and forthright. The knights agreed to pay a small fee for the space in the vault their gold would occupy. In order to keep track of what belonged to whom, each knight was given one hundred receipts, one for each piece of gold they deposited in the vault. One day, an inventor came to the noble and asked for some gold to develop his new brilliant idea he called electricity and light bulbs. The noble thought about it. He couldn't give out the knights' gold because they would surely kill him if they found out. He did not want to risk his own gold on the word of this stranger he did not know. He would want to own the electricity and light bulbs should they work. He resolved to play it safe, and he created a trap. He wrote receipts for which he had no deposits, knowing no one but him would know. This way, he really only risked some paper and ink. The noble handed the receipts to the inventor along with a contract for the inventor to repay this "loan" with "interest." Having no other choice, the inventor agreed to repay plus interest. Sometime later, having constructed their own vaults, all the knights came to collect their gold stored in the noble's vault. They traded in their receipts (cash) for the gold, save what was justly agreed upon as a fee. The noble, still being noble and true to his word in the eyes of the knights, now had all the receipts (cash) he made, a small amount of gold (fees paid), and a contract (loan) to the inventor. The next day, the inventor came to pay back the loan, and it was no surprise to the noble that he could not repay the loan interest. He had the electricity and light bulbs, they worked fine, but he could not cover the interest. "Since you cannot honor your word as I do, you have defaulted on your loan, and I claim ownership of your electricity and light bulbs," said the noble. Having no choice and feeling cheated, the inventor reluctantly agreed to give up his right to his marvelous invention, and all the control and profits it would yield.

The end.

So why would someone of "nobility" risk his good name and family honor on such a dubious affair? Perhaps it was for a really good idea that could change the world and offer expanded power and influence! Certainly, the benefit was well worth a little extra paper in the streets. Who's to know? The noble might think, *And when he can't repay the loan, because I haven't made the money (cash) for it, I will claim ownership of electricity and light bulbs—not by noble right or the sweat of my brow, but by common law. Agreeable to all, the common law.*

The "Tale of 100 Knights" is a generalization of the true function of a banking system—to conjure ownership of everything and everyone and to control everything everyone is ever going to do. And what the bank cannot own it seems to destroy. It also reveals the structure of fraud associated with creating money from debt. If all the banks seize all the deposits and confiscate all the property in the world, there would still be outstanding debt in the form of interest.

The single continuous thread between all the wars, suffering (slavery, starvation, and poverty), and crime in the history of the world is the debt money system. It is corrupt in nature from its creation. The moment the owner of the first vault wrote receipts for deposits (cash) he knowingly did not have, he was committing fraud by counterfeiting his own cash currency. He concealed this fraud by calling it a loan. He further had to justify his fraud by demanding profit in the form of interest, which he did not write a receipt (print cash) for.

*If you build a system based on corruption, corruption proliferates.*

Where is the cash to cover the interest supposed to come from? The bank will tell you to seek it out from your neighbors. They don't care where you get it from. So you have some choices: you can steal it (robbery/burglary, identity theft), sell something you already own or can make if you can find a buyer (sex industry, drug trade, black market goods, commercial/retail and yard sales), do extra work for it (labor for others, the fruits of which you may not own, slavery), "convince" your neighbor to just give it to you (fraud, larceny, big and little con games, begging), or try to make your own paper cash (criminal counterfeiting).

*Corruption results in economic and political instability and a lack of confidence among the populace.* In this book, I will introduce you to some new applications of old ideas that create a free and fair economic system based on the fundamental truth that your labor is your most sacred property and is the source of all wealth. I will describe how it is possible for every individual to own and profit from their labor, debt-free (Appendix).

## Crossroads

As long as we continue to support the for-profit, debt-based system, we are all supporting our own slavery and death. If we want peace and freedom, we have to do something different than returning to the gold standard and restarting the same old cycle all over again. We have to claim ownership of our present and future labor through a *nonprofit central bank (NPCB)*.

As time marches on, the scoundrels expand their influence. They are reaching farther and farther into our lives. They invade our privacy online, over the phone, in our homes, and at our jobs. More and more communication services are being distilled down to only one provider. The banking industry is whittling down to just one bank. Through direct deposit and automatic payments, they are taking control of your personal cash flow. Credit cards may see you through to ends meet, but credit cards just mean longer time in servitude. There is only one source of news and information, and it wears many different media labels. More and more countries are becoming trapped by and indebted to the World Bank. Global trade is becoming monopolized. Labor unions are being systematically dismantled. You are being asked to work harder, longer days with less pay and fewer, if any, benefits. Shit! You feel fortunate to just have a job. The financial burdens facing the majority of people are unnecessarily overwhelming. It is just getting worse. Soon they will eliminate the last bastion of freedom, cash, and when that happens, it's all over. You will be as cattle, penned in the corral of your town. Any hope of doing what you really love to will be gone. Following your bliss will seem like a sick joke. Your miserable days will run together until you die alone from an empty heart.

Yes, globalization will happen, but we still have a choice. Right now, the best strategy to reverse disaster is to beat them to the punch. If we can globalize ourselves first in a free and fair system like the NPBC, then we can seize our freedom, our bliss, our joy and, by our love of life, exalt it high through the ages. I still believe in life, liberty, and the pursuit of happiness and justice for all.

Right now, the only choice most of us have is to live as a slave or die. The NPCB alternative can globalize the people under real freedom, compassion, and dignity instead of humiliation, slavery, and oppression. All that is needed is the right contract and some software. The contracts already exist; they just need some small tweaks. The software already exists; it just needs some small tweaks. We can pounce on this opportunity and use all the same rules, laws, and policies being used to suppress and enslave us and redirect them to liberate and free all of humanity in peace and prosperity for the rest of time.

The solution to this glorified loan shark of a banking system is for the people to create money with the only thing we naturally possess, the same thing that gives money its actual value, our labor. *Debt-free labor as money is the key to global freedom and global sustainability.*

## Why Should I Support a Nonprofit Central Bank?

A public nonprofit central bank will

- stabilize the current financial system forever without possibility of collapse;
- eliminate the possibility of default on debt;
- eliminate unemployment;
- eliminate the economic disadvantages that motivate human migration for financial reasons;
- greatly reduce the immigration problems faced by First World nations;
- eliminate the motivation for most crimes, save crimes of passion;
- greatly reduce the financial motivation for the average person to participate in warfare;
- provide a stable and profitable platform for infrastructure, public health care, education, environmental stewardship, endangered species preservation, and retirement to name a few highly beneficial but as yet not profitable sectors of global concern; and
- establish and secure real, practical freedom of life, liberty, and the pursuit of happiness.

A NPCB system will foster and support these beneficial scenarios...

1. Every person will have *productive value* in the system. Every person will have the ability to produce goods and services that will provide individual wealth and collective value.
   a. Wars and property destruction will be detrimental to the unlimited profit produced by the NPCB. Presently, numerous wars are being financed by for-profit banks and enabled by poverty of the participants and debt. Peace will become more profitable than war to the banks because of the NPCB.
   b. Unemployment is dissolved. The NPCB system gives everyone the power to convert their labor—the source

of all wealth—into money debt-free. It provides a method for everyone to be self-employed by default.
c. Poverty is dissolved. Empowered by the NPCB system, everyone has a means to earn a living with or without permission from an employer.
d. Hunger is satisfied. Because any labor is profitable, people will be able to grow as much food as they need for their families and communities and earn debt-free pay as they do it. Unarable land can be developed and farmed at a profit.
e. The need to immigrate will be greatly reduced. People are forced to leave financially disadvantaged and violent areas in search of paying work and safety. The NPCB system will enable anyone to earn money wherever they are. The least developed areas will have the greatest potential for earnings by development and therefore highest profit potential.
f. Because everyone will be able to make a living on their own in their preferred way, people will not be forced to commit unsavory acts in order to maintain subsistence. Crime involving money will be reduced worldwide. There will no longer be a financial motive for crimes such as prostitution or theft in all its forms.
g. The NPCB creates a positive feedback loop for the money supply without adding debt. This perpetual money supply will secure all present and future debt from any possibility of default.
h. These major problems with society and the world economy will be solved. The universal benefits of the NPCB system greatly outweigh the restricted payout to the neediest in the present system.
   i. People will finally have another inalienable source of income that they can use to pay off debts. If the people have the money to pay back the banks, then everything is fine. The people keep their property, and the banks stabilize and maintain their valua-

tion. Realistically, right now there will never be enough money to pay back the banks because the banks create more debt than they do actual money. If the banks were to seize all of the world's deposits and confiscate all the world's cash and gold, there would still be outstanding debt. The banks may own their currency, but they should not try to possess your property or labor.

ii. With an NPCB, the economy will have a stable foundation of active consumers. All the chaos and financial panic will evaporate because the people will have a stable system to earn enough money to meet their needs and pay their debts without obstacles.

2. Beneficial yet not presently profitable, humanitarian and environmental efforts will not only be fundable, but *profitable*. The world is at a tipping point. The fraudulent money systems are reaching the end of their cycle historically (2). The end of the age of Pisces is transitioning to the age of Aquarius. All the taxes collected are not enough to pay the interests on the global banking debts, and the private banks want to foreclose and claim ownership and possess the world. The economists are worried about overpopulation and how inadequate industrial farming will be able to feed everyone at a profit. Wars are being waged over more and more of the surface of the earth in addition to the oceans being poisoned by radiation and plastic trash. Climate change is accelerating, resulting in drastic weather conditions, volcanoes, hurricanes, tsunamis, defaults . . . Aaaaarrrgghh! The human race created most of this disaster, and we are the only thing that can stop the apocalypse. The world is a mess. The NPCB system makes cleaning it up possible, profitable, and sustainable. It mobilizes everyone in the world with the earning potential of their individual labor.

3. Globalization is going to happen. If we don't make any changes, they could stage a large war to kill off most of the people to reduce the population to more corporate manageable numbers. Under corporate dominion, they will force you to buy *their* water, eat *their* food, breathe *their* air, and do all *their* work. If nothing changes, it is very probable that the new world order will be global slavery (3). Do nothing, and your children might learn firsthand how hard it is to build a pyramid.
4. We, the *people*, can globalize ourselves first; put in place a benevolent money system that will liberate; enable everyone to follow their bliss, eliminate most crime, poverty, starvation; and fuel progress, environmental stewardship, and sustainability worldwide. Imagine a worldwide populace with enough money to meet their daily needs without a debt burden or tax obligation. Is it that hard to accept a world where every man and woman is free to own the fruits of all their labor? We all deserve a free, peaceful, clean, healthy world to live in.

# PART I

# Problems

## CHAPTER 1

# Banks

In order to better comprehend the banking system at large, we must consider the original motivation for banking in general.

Traditionally, a community bank was a service to the community. People of the community deposited their money in the bank for "safekeeping." The vault in a bank was considered safer than stuffing your money in the mattress because a flood or fire would not destroy it and it was a good deterrent for theft. It was generally understood that bank management would loan and invest money, presumably in order to support the community. It is not generally understood that the money for loans comes directly from everyone's deposits.

I always assumed the money for loans came from the bank's own money, collected from fees and interest payments. It wasn't until my late thirties that I realized that this money comes from the deposits themselves. In my early forties, I learned that the banks loan out way more money than they have account deposits for.

*Once you give your money to the bank, it's gone.*

If there ever comes a day when the bank has to go out of business, you will suddenly realize this truth: you gave your money away to the bank and now the bank won't give any of it back, and you can't have it any more.

You give it to them, and they take it and use it for loans and investments. They keep up appearances by making an individual record of how much you give and take from them and encourage you to do the same. This record of activity is known as an account: a tedious record of the ebb and flow of currency represented by positive and negative numbers associated with an actual (personal) or fictitious person's (business) financial affairs. The bank may add positive numbers (interest payments) to one's accounting based on arbitrary rules related to a small percentage of the average balance. An average balance is good for the bank because it represents an amount of currency that won't be withdrawn. If you give them money they know they can keep indefinitely (a minimum deposit/balance, certificate of deposit, savings bond), they reward you by paying various degrees of higher interest to help you feel good about giving your money away.

Your account record, passbook, checkbook, and related cards also serve to lure you into a false sense that you actually have money in a bank. You think you have money in the bank because your account balance says so. There is a lot of theater associated with an account (two forms of identification, fingerprints, chips, passwords, etc.) that aid the illusion that your money is real and really safe in the bank. As I mentioned earlier, once you give your money to a bank, it is really gone. You trade it for an accounting record, and the bank actually loans it away or puts it in their pockets as bonuses and dividends.

Originally, for the real people who had to try to keep track of this tedium by hand, efficiency was paramount. If there were ways to cut corners and do something once instead of ten times and get the same accurate result, then all the better.

As the communities grew, so did the number of accounts, loans, and investments the banks had to keep track of. It became impossible to balance the "big picture" of the bank so that there would be a clear total of money deposited to accounts, which would give rise to the total amount available for loans and investments on a daily basis. Before computers, they had to work by hand. The bank would have to first collect all of the tellers' receipts for deposits, withdrawals, payments, etc. Then it would have to subtract the amount of new loans issued for the day and hope they hadn't loaned more money than they actually had in reality.

*This is the genesis of the two-day hold.* As the volume of activity overwhelmed the accounting staff, they fell behind, and it would take them a couple of days to catch up.

Inevitably, the bank had to compartmentalize its functions and break internal communication in order to get through the day. It was "full steam ahead and damn the torpedoes." The loan officer did not have to worry about how much was actually in the collective accounts. He or she did not have to know how much they were able to loan responsibly. They just had to do the job and make the loan. The bank's management would bet that it all would eventually even out and no one would ever find out their money was actually gone and start a "run on the bank." (4)

It's easy to see how a busy bank in a large metropolitan area could be overwhelmed during times before computers and networking programs. It might take a week or two to do it accurately. After sorting out human errors, the numbers were obsolete because the next new day would change the financial landscape of the banks virtual vault. So the quarterly and annual summary reports were used to track and value the bank business for management and its investors.

So on any given day, the bank may have well loaned out way more money than it actually holds in deposits. The bank is actually borrowing from itself from day to day. It's business as usual if no one finds out that everyone's account money is actually spent. The bank just has to keep enough cash on hand to handle the daily activities at the teller windows. The jig is up, and the fraud is revealed if everyone tries to withdraw their money at the same time. Historically, this is called a "run" on the bank, because when you hear your money is gone, you run to the bank to get it. This is how the first large-scale banking failure happened. For some reason, this irresponsible system continues to this day.

But wait! If there was not enough money in the bank to loan out, where did the actual money for the loans that went out come from? I mean, if you have a pile of ten rocks and someone else wants thirty rocks, how can they drive their cart away with thirty rocks?

Answer: Because the real rocks have been replaced by paper with pictures on it that is easily printed on demand. Electronic numbers in computers networked together is even easier. Here is that efficiency propensity we mentioned earlier.

Money is literally created from loans (debt), not from controlled and carefully reasoned orders by the government as we are led to believe.

*Shouldn't that mean the bank is in debt to itself? If its bottom line is a negative number (more loans than deposits—overdrawn), then shouldn't it have to cover its loss from its profits rather than future deposits?*

If the average person gives out more than they take in, they have to earn more to make up the difference. If this happens to regular people, they are considered irresponsible and chided even by banks, especially by banks.

Ever since the Federal Reserve Act of 1913, (5) the banks turn to the *central bank*, or "the Fed," and borrow the difference overnight at what is famously known as *the prime interest rate*. Yes, the prime rate, the rate on which all other interest rates are indexed.

After the first large-scale banking failure in the United States, some bankers got together and created the third national bank, the central bank known as the Federal Reserve Bank, "the Fed," (6). This bank's job is to loan money to banks overnight to cover the negative number of a bank's overall balance between deposits and loans. This money is loaned from the Fed with interest attached to all of the banks in the country. The Fed also loans all the US dollars printed by the US treasury to the US treasury, with interest attached. This is the national debt. The US treasury owes the Fed.

All the banks in the country had to join this federal reserve system and pay $100,000 (circa 1913 dollars) for the privilege of joining this private club or face government-enforced fines of $100,000 a month. This is when the government officially started working for the bank and why people think the Federal Reserve Bank is a government bank like the US treasury when in fact it is a private bank with private interests and private owners. The same system is set up for the World Bank and the International Monetary Fund (IMF). All the other banks in the federal reserve system are indebted to the Fed.

The federal reserve system is organized into several reserve banks, each with its own region like a fiefdom. The rules and guidelines the reserve banks use to govern the other banks is called the fractional reserve banking system (5).

Wait! Where does the money the Fed loans to the banks come from? The answer is the computer software, originally from a check from the US treasury with no account number on it. Money is created with loan contracts (2). The US treasury creates a bond (IOU) from everyone's birth certificates (7). That bond is used as collateral for the national debt. *Why does the US treasury have to borrow money from the Fed when it prints the money it borrows from the Fed?*

This bond IOU is based on the projected taxes and fees the government expects to collect over the lifetime of the individual (valued at around US$650,000). The bond number is the unexplained number in red ink on the back of your actual birth certificate. The government promises all the taxes and fees it "guesstimates" it can collect to the central bank as collateral on the loan of fresh money. No wonder the bank acts like it owns everything and everyone. The government has basically sold everything public and private to the bank as collateral for the loan that creates the national debt!

Knowing this, it is easy to see how the central bank can leverage politicians into supporting wars, the drug trade, and other hurtful endeavors that are immensely profitable for the bank. Remember, if you use it as collateral for a loan, you have sold it to the bank and hope to buy it back. With perpetual debt, they government sells the revenue you're expected to generate from your labor to the private central bank with no intention of buying it back. The bank will eventually try to claim ownership of all your labor (revenue). It is all about ownership. This idea brings new depth the term *debt slave*.

The Fed is the central bank and uses debt to create money. This money is created without risk to the Fed to cover the negative number held overnight by smaller banks that have created more money with loans than they had reserves in deposit. I am referring to the "fractional reserve" system of the Federal Reserve Bank system (5). This system says that member banks can loan out 90 to 95 percent (they set their own reserve rates) of the amount of money they have in deposit in checking accounts. *That's why banks always push you to get a checking account.* This leaves a small reserve of cash on hand to handle the daily ins and outs at the teller counter. If the member bank loans out over the reserve limit, which it easily and frequently does, the Fed automatically loans the reserve balance overnight with interest. *It is impossible to audit the Fed!* It would come as no surprise to me if the currency the Fed loans the member banks overnight is created from thin air.

By creating money with debt, a cruel and unnecessary shortage is also created. Instead of making it easy for anyone participating in this charade to get a loan, the accounting firm Fair, Isaac and Company (FICO) has created an algorithm that favors those who already have surplus money and don't need to borrow.

They do this by awarding points to those who choose to maintain a running debt and have little or no possibility of missing a scheduled payment. This number is called your credit score and every bank, merchant, and account holder is now part of this system. If you pay off all your debts, it actually lowers your FICO score. Your score will rise only if you can maintain perpetual debt on schedule (8).

*One can only maintain perpetual debt if one has a surplus of funds and thus no need for credit in the first place.* Clearly, this crooked game keeps money available only to those who already have it and next to impossible to get for those who need it. This institutionalized shortage is responsible for all crimes (save for crimes of passion) as well as poverty, squalor, and starvation worldwide. The only reason to create money with debt is to give unfair advantage to the creator and establish a later claim to ownership.

In this system, a *nonprofit central bank* could loan to member banks debt-free.

# Money

*It is all make-believe.*

From the beginning of our existence on this beautiful planet we call earth, everyone had to provide what they needed for themselves. Intricately tied to the earth, an individual had to grow and hunt for his or her own food, make their own clothing and shelter, collect water, domesticate animals, harvest crops, store crops, store seeds, pass on what they learned along the way, educate their young, and research and develop better ways to do everything. They soon learned that if they divided up labor, prioritized tasks, and specialized, everything got better. Farmers were able to yield more and more crops when that was all they had to do. Clothiers produced finer thread and warmer fabrics when that was all they had to do. Cooks made better meals for everyone when that was all they had to do.

Families grew larger and grouped together to form communities. If they were happy, they elected leaders to manage the resources and respond to emergencies.

Communities were isolated and found out that they could enjoy things from beyond their lands by trading with travelers. The things travelers could transport to trade were small and portable, like spices, jewelry, tools, and the like. Communities drew strength from trade. If the community did not have anything the traveler could use, no trade was made. If the community needed something in particular, it would send out travelers of their own with what they had to trade and returned with the needed or desired goods.

| Currency |
|---|
| Medium of exchange |
| Unit of account |
| Portable |
| Durable |
| Divisible |
| Fungible (interchangeable) |

| Money |
|---|
| Medium of exchange |
| Unit of account |
| Portable |
| Durable |
| Divisible |
| Fungible (interchangeable) |
| Store of value over time |

Credit: GoldSilver, *Hidden Secrets of Money* by Mike Maloney.

In time, the lazy and unhappy found that they could take by force the goods other travelers were carrying and use it themselves or trade without having to do the work of production. This led to ever-escalating crime (war), and the communities grew to city-states—walled off self-sustainable communities with security and a majority property owner.

This major property owner had many titles over time (like king, sultan, and Caesar) and created a medium of exchange to make trade easier for everyone within his walls. This medium has evolved over time from crops like tobacco to salt, cowry shells, iron bars, and other metal of mythical power that were symbolic of prosperity—such as gold, which had never-ending luster, and silver, which has properties of purification.

Eventually, these metals were pressed into uniform shapes we know as coins. An individual could collect coins from labor or trade and then trade them for goods and labor. This idea spread and became the norm of human interaction. If you want food, you buy seeds to plant and then grow and harvest or buy already-made bread for a little more. Every city-state had its own coins and applied its own value to them. One coin could be traded for a cart of wheat here or just a loaf of bread there. People became liberated from the biological demands of the earth and her bounty.

This also created slavery (free labor) and the demand for slaves. Slaves are chiefly an economic class of people who work but cannot own, who harvest but cannot sell, who are considered the property of others and can be bought and sold. The only compensation for their labor is crude shelter and bottom-rate food. They are conveniently distinguished by their physical differences of appearance, like skin color, facial features, and the language they speak, with their value being determined by the volume and type of labor they can perform.

Then the coin became the motivating force for human life. To dig the metal for coins, to grow crops, to raise cattle, to build, to create, and to destroy were all for and by the coin. To have coin meant freedom; to be without it meant slavery. Today, coins are no longer even made of quality metals. They are counterfeit tokens of implied value applied by the lenders, which is known as legal tender or currency.

*Ultimately, the value of money is applied by mutual agreement—make-believe.*

## A CURE FOR SLAVERY

The merchant asks so much for a product, and the consumer pays that amount or haggles for a more agreeable price. If consumers continuously cannot or will not pay the asking price, the merchant must take a lower price in order to move products. If everyone agrees that a coin could be fairly traded for a wagon, then the price is one coin a wagon. The price of the wagon does not change because its value is subjective. One person may value the wagon highly as a mode of transportation; another may not care for the wagon at all and could not put it to use and therefore would not give it much value. The idea of value is just that—an idea.

The market of the city-state blew up to engulf the entire world and became the world market economy. The more you have of something, the less value it has, even gold or people. For the super rich, money has little value. For the super poor, money has more value than life itself. They are willing to kill for it. The value of money is proportional to the amount available to you. The only thing keeping money valuable is the artificial shortage created by the structure of the banking system now.

Under the gold standard, the shortage is real, as there is a limited amount of gold in use. Without being limited by the gold standard, currency is created at will by the banks and is therefore unlimited. Any shortage of unlimited imaginary money is artificial and deliberate.

As the importance of money increases in your life, your individual freedom erodes, and you become enslaved to the financial system known as the "free" market economy. To have coin is freedom; to not have coin is slavery.

They tell you in economics class that ESP is responsible for the loss of value of currency. People suddenly decide that this coin no longer purchases what it used to. They use reasons like it's not as well made as the previous coins or there is not enough gold or silver contained in the coin to give it the value it once had. Other factors are how well the wars are going and the availability of the product. We are told that gold will not loose its value because it will not tarnish. Modern coins will not tarnish either but are still not considered as valuable as gold.

The value of gold itself is variable. With the historically inevitable global financial collapse (loss of confidence in value) of currency, gold is projected to be priced at what is now US$20,000 per ounce (9). I am sure the holders of gold would love that price to go even higher, but these figures are ludicrous, and the value will be what will be agreed on by the individuals trading at the time of trade. In other words, we will have to see what it is when the time comes.

*Value* is best defined in my mind as "(noun) worth in usefulness or importance to the possessor, utility, or merit."

Somewhere along the line, the value of money in our lives became exaggerated and blown out of proportion. Perhaps it was the idea in the book *Second Treatise on Government* by John Locke (10) that one could use money to purchase labor in unlimited quantities. Or maybe it was Adam Smith's notion in his book *The Wealth of Nations*[1] that conveniently justified racism, slave trade, and poverty and proclaimed the system itself was godlike via "the invisible hand" (11). Throw Edward Bernays (12) into the mix with his ideas that spiritual satisfaction could be purchased with the correct primal triggers placed in advertising. Mix them all together, and you have a self-referring, self-justifying false-godlike system that justifies starvation, slavery, and murder.

I have heard that inflation of the currency supply will raise prices. This would suggest that every merchant has a running total of the entire money supply in the back of their heads, and when it increases, they have to raise their prices to match. In my experience, when I asked a merchant why their prices went up, I have never been told it was because the money supply increased. It's always some other factor directly affecting the merchants' costs, like higher gas prices affecting delivery fees, resource scarcity, or exchange rate fluctuations; it was never because there is more money available for

---

[1] "Every species of animal naturally multiplies in proportion to the means of their subsistence, and no species can ever multiply beyond it. But in civilized society, it is only among the inferior ranks of people that the scantiness of subsistence can set limits to the further multiplication of the human species; and it can do so in no other way than by destroying a great part of the children which their fruitful marriages produce." Adam Smith-The Wealth of Nations.

circulation. I believe the inflation of prices is due to manipulation by the invisible hand than to currency inflation.

The US treasury will invest the bond created from your birth certificates in the stock market where the invisible hand ensures they are profitable or not. However, you, the commodity that bond is created from, are not entitled to any of the profits.

"It takes money to make money" means that a kind of permission is required. If you don't have any money, either you can't make it or it is extremely difficult to make any money without permission. The permission comes in the form of employment, bank loan, and government grant (or angel investor). This artificial reality creates a closed club for those that have money and excludes those who don't. Only the favored or those who prove useful to the furtherance of control are allowed to make money of influence. This mechanism of control is the source of poverty, crime, vices, and most of the ills of our beautiful world. It is a function of the invisible hand.

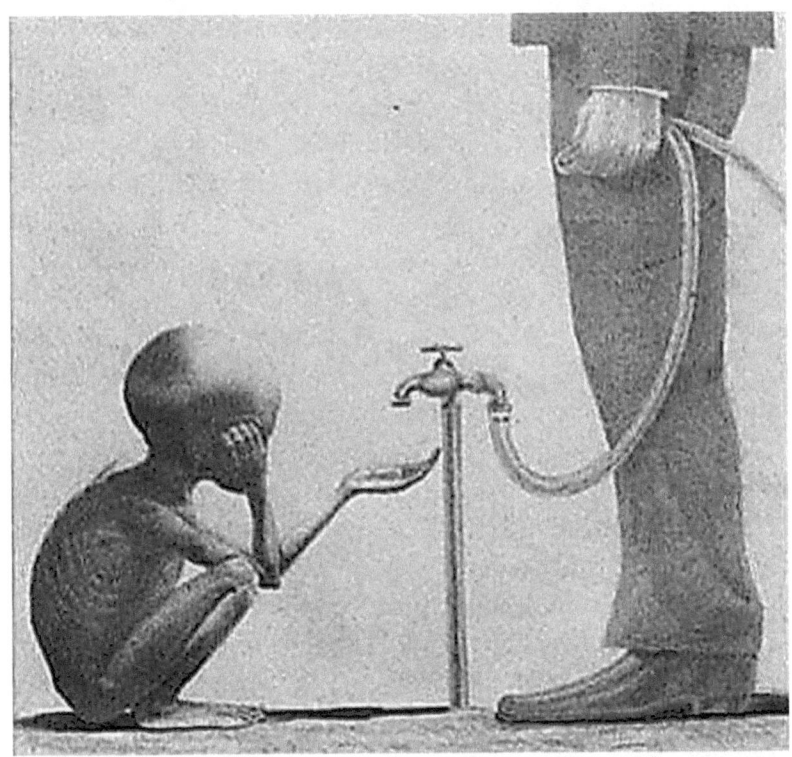

## Interest

"Interest: an excess above what is due or expected" (*Miriam-Webster Dictionary*).

The banking scheme feeds on the promise of gain without labor. When banks were numerous and community oriented, there was competition, and they would attract customers by promising to pay the depositor interest on the amount of money they chose to deposit. In the 1940s, 2 percent on savings was sold as a generous consideration in the USA. Banks would also compete against one another by charging lower interest rates on loans and paying higher rates on accounts than the competition. Depending on how badly the money was needed by the individual and how popular the home, auto, or unsecured credit loan product was at the time, 6 percent, 10 percent, or 15 percent were not uncommon loan rates in the early '90s.

Loan sharking is considered a crime. It's called *usury*. That is when the lender takes unfair advantage of the person's misfortunes and makes an unethical or immoral loan. An unethical loan to me would be to loan money to someone who cannot possibly pay it back. An immoral loan to me would be to charge high interest rates and demand large frequent payments. Under the law, both of these harmful loans are considered *usury*.

Almost every religion condemns usury as a sin. In some religions, it is forbidden to loan money at interest at all. Others only forbid charging interest to fellow followers of the same faith. They could, however, charge interest to everyone else, and that is probably the motivation behind a lot of religious persecution people have endured (13). Philosophers like Plato and Aristotle spoke out against charging interest because it is harmful.

Over time monarchies, churches, and governments permitted usury within reason. Relatively low interest rates and proof of the person's ability to repay the loan were required to receive a lawful loan from a bank. If your situation was desperate, you could always see a loan shark, a private person usually connected to organized crime, and get your loan and the stereotypical bodily injury when you missed your ever-increasing payments.

When a bank loan is made, there are two parts: first is the principal, which is the actual amount of money created, and second is the interest, which exists only as an idea. Interest benefits only the lender. Imagine all the money in a country as a commodity, like gold coins. Now imagine that a person lends out ten coins and he or she is asking twelve in return. This is a 20 percent interest rate. Let's say the loan gets repaid and now the lender has twelve coins and then loans out the same ten coins but buries the two coins received as an interest payment.

Continue this process, and if there were one hundred coins in the realm and two coins fall from circulation with every loan completion (recession), there can only be forty-five or so loans made before the lender has buried most of the gold coins in the realm (depression). The next loan of ten gold coins cannot have the expected interest paid as the coins are not available within the whole realm (bankruptcy). Then the lender can claim ownership of the borrower's property in lieu of the interest coins (default). If the lender is allowed to create paper currency as a loan to the governing body of the realm and issue that instead of gold coins to the people and then ask even higher interest, it is still only a matter of time before the lender can claim ownership of the realm by default. It is a con game. The governing body of the realm can create its own substitute coins, a process called hyperinflation of the money supply, but historically, it just proves to delay the inevitable rather than solve the problem.

That is why usury is a crime and a religious sin. What happens to everyone else, except the lender, when they have no property or money? What is to be done with the wretched masses? Perhaps it would be convenient for the lender if the wretched just killed one another in a war rather than the scheme being revealed and the lender being driven out of the realm (13). Or perhaps the lender could put everyone to work building a large stone pyramid as a monument to his triumph and pay them with food rather than coin. Interest debt is the source of discontent and the evil aspect of money.

The interest rate is the rate at which money and property are transferred to the lender over time. At the time of this writing, amazingly, there are interest rates as high as 60 percent in Russia. Another way to look at it is this: Imagine all the monetized wealth of a given body (city, country, or world) as a lake of water. At the bottom of the lake is a drain pipe called interest. The interest rate is relative to the diameter of the drain pipe. The higher the interest rate, the bigger the pipe, the faster the wealth drains out of the collective populace.

*Debt currency is hollow.*

Nowadays, all currencies are created by a loan with interest. There is always more interest owed than currency created. That's why it is impossible to repay the national debt in the United States or anywhere else they use debt to create currency. Without real commodity or gold or silver money, the only thing giving currency value is the collective imagination and property of the masses, especially their labor.

Real commodity or gold or silver money are themselves impractical for use as a stable money supply because of supply limitations. The hard reality is, there will always come a time when the economy needs more physical gold than it has supply for. Because we are human, we cheat and hyperinflate the currency for convenience and function. The cycle starts as commodity money (9); necessity converts it to currency and then to hyperinflated currency. From here, the ESP of the populace losses confidence in the hyperinflated currency, and the system collapses and returns to commodity money. This cycle has repeated again and again for thousands of years simply because commodity money, like gold or silver, cannot be supplied in sufficient quantities to grow with development. This inflexibility aspect of gold and silver necessitates the need to inflate to match demand in the first place. The crime comes from using debt and interest for private gain as a mechanism for creating new public currency (2).

The obvious solution to the debt problem is currency created debt-free throughout the collective populace. The currency can be more stable and reliable than commodity money if it is based on the real foundation of all wealth—labor. A labor standard for currency creation will automatically grow with development. As the population grows, so does the money supply to match.

# CHAPTER 2

# Labor

*Labor is your most sacred property!*
   Butchers' Union Co. v. Crescent City Co., 111 U.S. 746 (1884) defines labor as property—and the most sacred kind of property. "Among these unalienable rights, as proclaimed in the Declaration of Independence is the right of men to pursue their happiness, by which is meant, the right any lawful business or vocation, in any manner not inconsistent with the equal rights of others, which may increase their prosperity or develop their faculties, so as to give them their highest enjoyment . . . It has been well said that *'the property which every man has is his own labor, as it is the original foundation of all other property so it is the most sacred and inviolable'*" (emphasis mine).
   "All wealth is the result of labor" (John Locke).
   Which comes first—the labor or the gold? All money is the result of labor. Labor dug it out of the ground, labor smelted and refined it, labor minted the coins, and labor carries it around and trades it for goods and services. If you mine for gold, strike gold, and then trade it for currency; you then become one of the few that can say they actually own their labor.
   Most of us give our labor to employers that trade debt-laden (hollow) currency in return. While we are employed, we cannot own anything we do or make while we are in service to the employer.

There is not one company I have worked for that did not require me to give up ownership of my labor by insisting I sign a form that says anything I create, make, or build while employed at that company is the company's property. Technically, all my ideas, hobbies, and interests became the company's property. They say that you have a choice not to sign that condition. However, if you do not sign, you do not get the job; therefore, there is no choice.

*Labor is like the power supply of the economy.* If you look at the economy like an electronic motor, the various sectors of labor would be copper coils, the magnets, the batteries, gears, axels and pulleys of the economic engine. The strength of the economy is like the horsepower and torque of an engine. The rate of consumption is proportional to the RPM or speed of the running motor. When the consumer base of the market cannot consume, the economy slows like an underpowered motor under heavy load.

The workers are the largest portion of the business organization, the population, and the consumer base of the economy. Underpaid workers cannot consume beyond subsistence, and the economy stagnates. Overpaid workers will consume abundantly, and the economy will surge.

Inadequate pay makes work destructive of one's mind, body, and spirit. Work is all-consuming of both time and attention as well as antagonistic to happiness if the results of your efforts are unsatisfying, fruitless.

The time of our lives is all we have. To me, the purpose of this short time is for people to express themselves in any way they see fit. This freedom of expression is the jewel of life and happiness. If free expression is suppressed, you have no freedom.

Oppression is the enemy of freedom. If our freedom of expression becomes oppressed by mundane labor performed to barely provide for the cost of living, then we are no longer free or happy.

The point of business, labor, and the entire economy is to facilitate happiness for all. That is freedom. If the cost of living exceeds the wages paid to labor, then the economic engine fails just like a machine with a dead battery. No power, no function. Labor is the foundation of economic power, like the materials of a battery or generator. Currency is like the flow of electrons in electric current. The community and government are the circuit board. For a machine to function well and exceed the demands placed on it, it needs a reliable, strong power supply. Business is the framework, currency is the electricity, and labor is the power source and mechanism. If a strong economy is the goal, then a strong base of consumption must be maintained; therefore, wages must be maximized.

As mentioned earlier, the pursuit of happiness is the primary course of freedom. The vehicle of happiness shared by everyone is facilitated by the economy. This vehicle provides the desirable comforts of home, as well as education, health care, safety, security, and the means with which to discover and seek out happiness (14).

*If you make it, it's yours!*

You naturally own your labor. If you make it, it's actually yours. If you paint a picture, you say, "It's my painting" until you sell it or give it away. While you were painting your picture, you decided everything about it from the materials, the location, the tools, and the amount of time and effort you put into your work. It is entirely your creation; you own every bit of it. In a lot of ways, it is a part of you.

Slavery is when you do not own your labor. It is not your labor if you have very limited influence in the choices of time and effort, materials, location, tools, design, and organization. The only thing you have to contribute to an employer is obedience. By obedience, I mean cooperation and some effort. You show up on time in the correct costume as instructed and intake, generate, sort, and move papers or products for a scheduled amount of time in order to receive some currency compensation in the future. You are playing the game. You need permission to play the game from an employer or an investor if you want to run your own game. You have to play the game because you need money to live. Time and effort are the only things you have to trade for currency.

If you sell your labor as time and effort, then you are known to be employed. If you give your labor away, then you are a volunteer. If you keep your labor and delight in the fruits it bears, then you are free. If you do not receive what you value for your labor or time and effort, then you made a bad bargain. Did you really have a choice? If you are swindled and receive nothing for your labor, you are probably honest. If you allow yourself to be convinced that you could not possibly own your labor, then you are a fool. If your labor is coerced or forced from you without real choice and you receive little or nothing in return, then you are a slave. Iron chains have become the cost-of-living expenses and jobs with good benefits; the sting of the whip comes in the form of monthly bills and societal pressure to shop until you drop.

CHAPTER 3

# Economy

It has become clear to me that almost everything we have been taught about economics sounds marginally acceptable in theory and almost completely false in practice[2] (1)—for example, supply and demand. We were taught that supply and demand are the two things that relate to each other in some ideally balanced way and presumably influence prices and product availability.

The theory is that if there is a large supply of beds, for example, and demand for beds has remained constant, then the price of beds would go down. If the price goes down below what it costs the business to buy, store, and sell the bed, the business is spending more than it takes in and will fail in a competitive market. In order to cure the imbalance, the price of beds would be dropped far enough to inspire even the most frugal of customers to buy a bed even if they didn't need one. The price could even drop below cost temporarily. In this example, the pricing of beds related to demand is a retail deci-

---

[2]  "FIRST PRINCIPLE: 'Economics' is an intellectual Trojan horse with political agendas hidden within known-false assumptions. The political conclusions follow *logically* from the assumptions, so if you accept those known-false assumptions, then you also accept those hidden political agendas" (Jay Hanson).

sion that is absent of all consideration of the overall national money supply.

The problem here is the subjectivity of pricing related to demand. Demand is subjectively limited to specific markets or certain parts of the population grouped into different categories or demographics. For example, teenagers will not usually need to purchase adult diapers. The price is determined by what will move the most products in the least amount of time. Sales comparisons from the past are used to measure the present performance of management, sales staff, and product performance.

All this activity is divided into blocks of time, such as the quarter (three months). The quarter is what is frequently used to determine if a business is making money or not. It seems they need such short blocks of time in order to respond to system failures or influence of the invisible hand. Such system failures have been creatively labeled with terms like *market volatility* and *self-correction*. Some doubt creeps in from subjective and sometimes irrational methodology of pricing related to demand. Take the example above; selling the mattress below cost or offering to pay 120 percent of the asking price of a residential property regardless of the actual value of the property, for instance, does not follow practical business sense.

## Demand Can Be Artificial or Real

Artificial demand is created by a mind-set or collection of isolated numerical data detached from the whole. For instance, in the beds example, the price of beds is low because the retailer has more beds than he or she wants. Perhaps the beds are secretly defective or have an unpopular color or the sign in front of the store is damaged, which gives the establishment an undesirable appearance and customers don't come in. So in order to reduce the inventory of beds to the desired amount and attract customers, they lower the price to inspire consumption. Even if this price is below the retailers' cost or even cost of manufacture, they have decided that these beds must go. Businesswise, selling below cost at any time is not profitable and appears to be plain, poor business in the long run.

## A CURE FOR SLAVERY

In the short-term shell game of business, sometimes a little razzle-dazzle is necessary. Perhaps the business is cash poor at the moment and needs a cash injection to cover short term bills, even payroll. The objective of business is to have more money than you started out with at the end of the time period—which, for sake of this discussion, is the quarter.

Let's continue. So this low price of beds automatically creates a demand. We have been taught that a low price is good and that we should spend to buy at a low price as a principal. This only makes practical sense if (1) you need a new bed anyway and/or (2) you're going to resell the bed at the standard and usual price in a different consumer demographic (market) to collect a profit. That is free enterprise.

The retailer can use this loss in an abstract way. It can use the artificially high number of beds or units moved (detached from price, of course) in reports to show how successful or vibrant the business is to attract investors, sell stock, or appease superiors within the organization. "Last quarter our business grew by x percent because we moved y percent more units than the previous quarter." No matter how pretty they want to dress it up, it is still a loss overall. It's all make-believe.

To solve the problem of stagnant demand, they have very powerful media to manufacture need in the consumers' minds (15). They show you, the consumer, unrealistic characters doing things in carefully constructed advertisements to trigger a subconscious and/or primal response like fear, lust, or passion so you do not feel complete or desirable or happy unless you have this thing they want to sell. It works very well—so well that now we have gotten to the point that every quarter there is something new to buy. We have been conditioned so that if we don't have a new one, we feel somehow deficient. You have been conditioned to look at others as deficient if they do not have new things.

This is not demand; it's mind control by the media. Computers and TV are your invisible hand puppeteers. When the banks enable this behavior with readily available fresh money in the form of credit cards, you become as cattle nosing up to the trough. You are no longer free; you are kept via debt in a prison created in your mind by the media.

## Real Demand Is a Need by Circumstance

Real demand is the circumstance that business exploits in order to exist. You are "selling water in the desert," for example. This is capitalism. This economic ideology of supply and demand is feeble at best. It can never be sustainable, as once everyone has a bed, the demand goes down.

Demand is transient, seasonal, and intermittent. Business has gotten very good at artificially creating demand to stay in business. This has resulted in lower-quality products designed and produced with planned obsolescence paramount, a.k.a. designed for the dump. If the bed is made to fall apart, then the consumer will need to buy a new one sooner rather than later.

To work around the transient nature of real demand and to create artificially sustainable demand is a foolish solution. It is a self-serving extreme that squanders resources at the expense of consumer trust and confidence and environmental integrity. It harms the community and the country when products fall apart rapidly and bloat the landfills and oceans.

Sustainable demand provides an idea that the business will stay active (profitable?) over more consecutive quarters. This illusion may look good to the accountants, but the reality is that limited resources are being processed into large volumes of unusable waste that are just going to the landfill. When the bed falls apart, the consumer throws it away. What happens to the business when there are no more beds available from the manufacturer?

Not only does this process use up our natural resources at an ever-expanding rate, but it also creates an unstable foundation for society. "It is a fool that builds his house upon the sand." Just look at any commercial district. Do you notice how many businesses open and close along the streets? It's always changing, like the dunes in a desert.

I absolutely hate it when I go to use something and it immediately breaks. Look around the room you are in right now. Imagine that everything you see will fall apart sooner rather than later and need to be replaced. How many times will you replace the entire contents of your house and perhaps even the house itself in your lifetime? Guesstimate the cost. I saw one infographic that says the average household contains US$30,000 of stuff that will need to be replaced every six months on average. Now imagine if you had that money to use for something more worthwhile.

Furthermore, demand can be artificially created with a little help from the bank by making debt available to both the business and the consumer in the form of credit loans, commonly known as credit cards. To the consumer, this is free money up front for a small monthly fee. Unbeknownst to most, this fee is amortized for fifteen years usually. "Would you take a bed today if you didn't have to pay for it until next year?" or "Would you take a bed today if we gave you a card to pay for it?" or still "How would you like to finance your fabulous new bed?" All this plays on the gullibility of the consumer that they will be getting something for what seems like nothing (make-believe). Factor in planned obsolescence, and you will still be paying for that bed long after you replace it. How many beds will you be paying for while you can sleep on only one at a time? Most, if not all, of the business in the United States run on credit.

Some more fallacious economic principles sound reasonable on the surface but fail to ring true upon close inspection.

*People choose; they seek to obtain the best possible combination of cost and benefit.* False. Before Edward Bernays, people always purchased only what they needed. Edward Bernase, the nephew of Sigmund Freud, convinced people through media manipulation and advertising that they will feel happier if they buy what they don't need as an "expression of their individuality." The consumer is manipulated into making a decision between products they ordinarily don't need or want.

*Scarcity.* False. It is not always naturally occurring in the global market; rather, it is more likely a result of the invisible hand manipulating commodities, prices, futures, stocks, currency exchange rates, etc., for profit (Enron).

*Opportunity cost—when we choose one thing, we refuse something else.* False. This is an example of all-or-nothing thinking, a cognitive distortion identified by Dr. David Burns. It is possible to have everything you need or want. Rich people do it all the time.

*People respond to incentives in predictable ways.* Sometimes true but not always—and not always for the monetary gain. Happiness is the best incentive. Everyone finds happiness in their own way.

*Economic systems influence individual choices and incentives. People cooperate and govern their actions through both written and unwritten rules. These rules determine what, how, and for whom a given product is produced.* False. More effects of the invisible hand self-referring. You can always make it yourself the way you want it and how you want it with what you have.

*The sole motivation of participation in the market is personal gain.* False. Most people participate because they are forced to by the system. Charitable donations fill the shelves in many nonprofit thrift stores. The donations were not for personal gain; consumption of donated goods is more an act of necessity rather than personal gain.

*The consequences of choices lie in the future; economists believe that the cost and benefits of decision-making appear in the future since it is only the future that we can influence. Sometimes our choices can lead to unintended consequences.* Translation: This mish-mash of fallacious ideas reaffirms our knowledge that we have no idea what we are doing. This also gives plausible deniability to the invisible hand for deliberate and malicious damages to the global financial system. "We didn't know it would to that . . ." Lie. We knew and we did it on purpose for our own gain (1). And it's all make-believe!

These economic principles serve the soulless, endlessly greedy, sociopathic, and psychotic business mentality that is a corporation. *However, most people are not psychotic corporations and just want to simply be happy.*

## Credit

*They tell you in an economy class that debt is good because without it, everything would stop.*

Nothing could be further from the truth. The truth is: debt is the excuse used to create new currency out of thin air for the purpose of coercing ownership of property.

So it is not debt that is good and necessary for the economy, but fresh new money. As I mentioned earlier, the economy runs almost entirely on credit.

Credit is basically money you can use and don't have to pay back right away. Another way to look at is this: *credit is money you can spend today and earn later* (make-believe).

Before you say, "I pay my credit cards off every month," let me explain that there are three kinds of credit: revolving, open, and installment (16). So while you are paying it off every month, you have open credit, which means you really don't need credit to live on and just use it for the convenience of not having to carry cash. You are not the majority.

Meanwhile, for the rest of the USA that is suffering under minimal wages and ever-inflating costs of living, revolving credit is the only lifeline. Revolving credit begins with a small amount of open credit or potential money limited by your amount of disposable income. It doesn't exist yet, but it can if you want it to. Once you use the card and buy something on credit, the money is created for the merchant, and you get to pay off the total amount of the purchase amortized or divided up over the next fifteen years, plus interest. The credit company will ask for a small payment every month. This payment is usually just the interest on the total. If you make your payments on time for long enough, they will reward you with a higher credit limit—not based on your disposable income, but now on your ability to maintain the debt on schedule. This reward reflects a boost to your FICO score. If you want to live the way the television tells you worthwhile people live and are not independently wealthy, revolving credit is the only game in town. Next time you go to the grocery store, notice how many people buy their groceries with a credit card signature.

Installment credit is something that is financed (like a car, house, or student loan) with monthly payments for a fixed amount of time. The actual money for these doesn't exist in reality until you sign the loan contract and agree to pay it back plus interest. Just the amount of the loan gets created by the keyboard, not the interest.

The pin number transaction is not credit; it is a debit or convenient access to your own money that the bank creates all kinds of games to block your access to and then charges you for it. Like me, I am sure many of you have been denied access to your money because of what I call "the available balance game" and then suffered a penalty for it via overdraft fees.

This is a throwback to preinformation superhighway conditions when checks had to be cleared by hand. They were mailed to the bank of origin, accounts were debited, and the merchant was paid by hand. Now the transactions clear instantly, and they purposely withhold your money from you for those two days or more so the bank can pad their loan pool and their operating capital on hand.

This is the fractional reserve banking available-balance game. They need to hold 10 percent of total deposits in reserve and loan out the rest. At the end of the day, if they have loaned out more than 90 percent of deposits, they are forced to borrow from the central bank, "the Fed," at the "prime rate" to cover their reserve requirements overnight.

They keep you from your money for those days to act as a buffer so they won't have to borrow so much. The bank uses your money to help save the bank money. To add insult to injury, this money in limbo is not available to anyone else, and they will return requests for payment as "NSF" or nonsufficient funds and charge you a penalty. This is short-term robbery in my mind, and any time the bank does not allow you access to your money, it is stolen.

Some of you may ask why the bank does this. The problem lies within the rules the banks created for themselves. As I mentioned earlier, it is called the fractional reserve banking system (2). Basically, the bank has given itself the power to create new money in the form of installment loan accounts (debt). For example, if the bank has $100 in deposits, they can create a $90 loan to a borrower. Then those $90 gets created by the signature on the agreement to repay and can be recorded as a deposit. Now they have $190 in deposits and can loan $171 from, which in turn can be counted as a deposit and loaned out, etcetera. Most of the bank's attention is focused on loan activity because of the huge implied profit ideation. So when you withdraw $200 to go shopping, it puts that deposit reserve in the red, and they might have to borrow from the Fed that night.

*This is the fraudulent core of the banking industry.*

The banks portend to have "noble" ethics—honesty and a "fiduciary responsibility." All the while, they are defrauding one another and everyone who deals with them. The fraud is evident in the fact that what is called a "run" on the bank is bad. If the bank was forthright, upstanding (noble), and actually had fiduciary responsibility, everyone could withdraw their deposits at the same time, and nothing would happen to the economy. After all, what's yours is yours, and what's theirs is theirs in a fair and honest system.

Credit cards are not included in the federal reserve system and do not have a reserve of deposits. I bet the actual currency used in a credit transaction does not really exist until you purchase a good or service with the card.

By using the card, you agree to pay back the principal plus interest. Again, only the principal amount of the price of the item is created with a programmed deposit to the merchant's account. The interest is created only in the idea of how much extra you have to repay, and a negative number is entered into your credit card account statement. With this system, it is possible to never be able to repay because of "capitalization."

Capitalization is the process where the amount of interest owed on a credit card account or other loan account is added to the principal and begins to accrue interest on itself or compound. This interest creating higher interest will keep you forever in debt if you need credit to live on. Capitalization is capitalism. To have coin is freedom; to not have coin is practical slavery.

Given the invisible hand's insatiable quest for ownership of everything, credit is the perfect vehicle to defraud you of your property, especially labor. Since it does not cost the banks anything but the paper the contracts are written on and the plastic for the cards, they carry no risk and offer no real consideration.

When you borrow from the bank with a loan or use a credit card, you are purchasing these items for the bank. You slowly buy these items back from the bank with your monthly payments. It's the same with your small business loan; you sold your business idea to the bank when you got the loan. Now, you get to work your idea for them until you either pay off the debt or drown under its ever-increasing weight. The more things that come into being via debt financing are more things the bank will try to claim ownership of eventually. All the financial bubbles that burst and stock markets that crashed happened when the banks tried to claim ownership of the fruits of their fraud.

*If you buy it with cash, you own and possess it immediately, and you only pay for it once.* Buy it with credit, and you will pay for it three or four times over. And the bank owns it—not you. You are essentially just renting it from the bank. Note: Remember, the credit score game rewards you with a high score to maintain perpetual debt instead of cures it by paying off your debts. In this way, you work for the bank to expand its ownership of whatever you possess.

## Fresh Money

The economy is entirely dependent on what I will call "fresh" money. Fresh money for the individual is a paycheck, a higher balance of available credit, investment dividends paid out, gifts of money received, inheritance, settlements, and anything else that puts money in one's pocket or on one's card. Fresh money for the economy at large (the national money supply) is created by the banks for the banks as debt owed by the government to the bank, using the people's private property (including labor) as collateral. The most recent vernacular for creating fresh money for the USA is *quantitative easing*.

## A CURE FOR SLAVERY

The idea that the economy is somehow supposed to function with a fixed amount of currency in circulation indefinitely is completely bogus. If that model were a person, they would be able to eat only their poop and drink their pee and live healthily forever. Fresh currency is like fresh food and water. It replenishes, nourishes, and provides energy for sustenance and growth. As it costs money to live (i.e., the cost of living), every day the individual spends or consumes money. Once this money is spent, it's gone like a sip of water swallowed.

In order to live, most organisms require fresh water every day. People require trips to the well, river, lake, stream, store, or tap for their daily supply. The financial aspect of an individual has the same requirement. Fresh money is required every day in order to thrive. If you are lucky, you receive your pail of fresh money (paycheck) once a week or biweekly, as most people do, or monthly or annually if you are less lucky. It all depends on how much fresh money you get and how often.

With luck, you frequently receive several times more money than you need to spend. Sometimes we call these lucky people rich. You are doing well if you receive enough to cover your cost of living and have enough left over to have some fun along the way and save some for a financial drought.

Most of the people of the world receive almost nothing once a month or a few times a year for daily work. I recall a news report of an impassioned plea for help in the form of a note from a Chinese worker that was concealed in the packaging of a Halloween decoration. He said they worked fifteen hours a day, seven days a week in a hostile work environment for $1.60 a month (17).

In the famine-stricken regions of Africa, that might be middle class. Every day thousands starve to death all over the world because they have no money to buy food. Contrary to popular belief, there is no food shortage; there is a money shortage—an artificial shortage of artificial currency.

# Debt

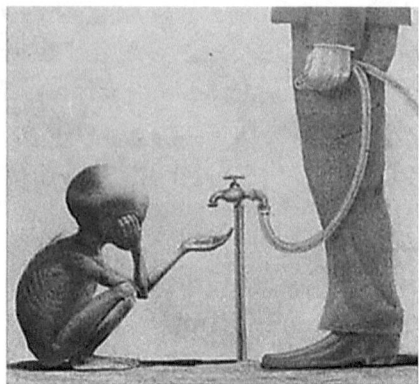

For the sake of this book, I will only consider the financial aspects of debt, an otherwise deep and vast philosophical idea. Debt is an obligation, a burden. Debt is also an accounting condition wherein sums of money that have already been spent require replacement by obligation.

This obligation is by agreement of the borrower—a bond. The lender creates the amounts borrowed by virtue of position. The actual currency is created out of thin air by computer key strokes with no loss to the lender. It does not cost the lender anything to create the currency being borrowed, but the borrower must labor to pay the sum borrowed plus the ever-growing interest. The borrower has use of the fixed amount of principal issued and must repay that plus the interest. The currency to cover the interest is never created. It is extra burden willfully inflicted on the borrower—punishment for not having enough money. "Woe to the conquered."

Financial debt becomes time in servitude. If you receive a student loan, you have to work to repay it. The old rhyme states, "I owe, I owe, it's off to work I go." The time required to serve is based on the amount of disposable wages that can be diverted to debt payments. The minimum payment will never relieve the burden of debt as the interest continues to grow. Most minimum payments are interest only and never reduce the actual amount borrowed (principal). *So one can labor and labor and never get out of debt.*

## A CURE FOR SLAVERY

Debt grows and grows exponentially with compounding of interest. This means that interest is being charged on interest. Another way to look at is time in servitude extended. This is basically slavery—involuntary servitude by flimflam and double talk, trickery. This would not be the case if the bank used its own money collected from fees to loans and investments. Instead it uses your money, my money, and everyone else's money to stuff its own pockets with. It creates financial hardships for people so they can do nothing else but work, work, and work and can't notice they have been swindled. The bank has written its own rules that allow it to create money with debt. It creates a lot of debt and, with interest, more debt than money (2). The more debt one acquires, the more time in labor one has to serve. As business strives to cut wages and benefits, the cost of living goes up and up, credit card debt goes up and up to make up the difference, and you have to work until the day you die. Is that freedom? Is that pursuit of happiness? I think not.

> How can the debt be paid? The only way to bridge the gap between the trailing currency supply and the leading debt is to create money debt-free. Because the currency to cover the interest doesn't exist, it is necessary to create it without creating additional interest debt (i.e., debt-free).

Because money is created by fraudulent debt and debt is time in servitude, the only value money has is labor. Money, when it was real gold, was a valuable commodity. Without intrinsic value, currency can only be valued by labor. Debt is modern slavery.

*If all the debt is repaid, everything will stop. False!*

Anyone with basic math skills can tell that fresh money is vital to the functioning of the economy and therefore society. The health of our entire society depends on the economy. The economy is a matter of national security. A healthy economy is dependent on consumption of goods and services. But to the economic organism, debt payment is a parasite on consumption. Debt is poison. The banking system creates more debt than currency when new currency is created via debt. The biggest demand for fresh currency is for consumption. Consumption is the heart of the body economic. If the economic body was an engine driving your pursuit of happiness, debt makes a one horsepower engine and two horsepower of load. If it were a biological cell, it would provide nutrients for one calorie of work and burn two calories to make it.

*Debt for the process of creating currency is a process of diminishing returns until failure—a negative feedback loop.*

The principal amounts of fresh currency created by debt for use are fixed and quickly consumed. Debt, on the other hand, is potentially eternal and grows exponentially via capitalization (compound interest). Compound interest is the biggest injustice in financial history. "Vie victize!" Woe to the conquered!

So it's not a surprise that time and time again, the budgets do not balance, the debt limit is raised, and bankruptcy and default are the status quo. There is no possible outcome other than failure.

The only problem with debt is that the holder of the debt tries to claim ownership of and possess the collateral—property and labor. Again, if all the banks seize all the deposits and all the properties, there would still be outstanding debt in the form of interest owed. *It is the bank's own fault they created a system wherein they cannot get paid.* In our modern time, the only collateral of any actual value is labor. To own another's labor makes a slave of the laborer.

When the ability of the general public to purchase things is reduced, they say the economy is in recession. Does that mean prices are going down? On some things maybe, but generally, no. If prices do drop, it is for a short time, and then prices will bounce back. When the public can easily and frequently buy things they do not need, the economy is said to be vibrant.

I have noticed that the economy is always kept on the edge of recession by various cost-of-living adjustments. If businesses are doing well, then the employees might be getting paid enough to save. Suddenly, the cost of transportation goes up with higher gas prices across the board, higher fines and fees, higher vehicle purchase prices, higher prime interest rates. If that doesn't sufficiently prevent people from saving, utility prices go up, the cost of education goes up, and the ever-present taxes are raised and collected with renewed vigor.

We have been taught that these cost-of-living increases are the result of conditions associated with the supply and demand principle and associated with inflation of the money supply. We are told that they are somehow inevitable and an unfortunate reality one must endure. In an age of such technological efficiency, this is an insult to one's intelligence.

## Bubbles

If business is doing really well and a lot of people are making a lot of money, the invisible hand generally gives it less than ten years before it is stopped, usually by a bank calling in debt. Look at the "roaring twenties," financed by stock market debt margin trading, which ended when the margin was called for no apparent reason in 1929. Look at the real estate bubble from 2000 to 2008 in the United States, financed by "no income, no job/assets" (ninja) (18) loans for real estate, which collapsed when the borrowers defaulted after the loans matured. All the investments purchased that were dependent on those mortgages imploded.

We have been taught that this is called a bubble, and we assume that bubbles burst naturally. There have been stock market bubbles, Internet bubbles, and real estate bubbles in recent memory, and they never pop by themselves.

Physical bubbles, like balloons and soap bubbles, do pop all by themselves. More often than not, physical soap bubbles pop when they come in contact with something. Is the bubble aware of the child?

*Economic bubbles are made and exist in a fictitious financial reality.*

Every aspect of financial bubbles are created and therefore controlled by banks. The bank creates the bubble with fraud. The bank bursts the bubble as the fraud is perfected (the in-and-in) (19). The people are yoked with the responsibility as a result.

The *visible* hand of the bank, the lenders with advertisements, can create bubbles with limitless fresh currency to serve its own profit interests.

*The invisible* hand is the fine print, the payment schedule, the balloon payments, the foreclosure proceedings—the finger that can burst the bubble. Is the borrower aware of the terms and his or her own financial abilities to pay? Is the borrower aware of the abilities of the invisible hand to destroy those abilities to pay at will?

This week you have a good job; next week, you don't. Have you ever been downsized, laid off, or had your position dissolved? Everything financial organization, business, corporation, paycheck is fluid like the sand. "It is a fool who builds his house upon the sand." When the bubbles burst, they do so to the advantage of the bank. The bank is the sand.

The amount of money counterfeited by the banks is staggering. Over $700 trillion in derivative contracts have been created.[3] It has been that way for over ten years now, so how come there isn't more inflation worldwide? Answer: Because the currency that has been created is tucked away in various digital compartments and is waiting to be laundered or collected as labor. Remember, without gold to base the currency on, labor is the only basis after real property. And with low, even slave, wages for labor worldwide, $700 trillion could buy generations of global labor.

The problem is, the criminal banks are trying to take possession of the United States, its people, and everything in it by using a default on the debt as a justifiable claim. The reality is, the national debt is a fraud. The bank offers no consideration for the debt as the currency is created from nothing but an IOU (2).

*To have a valid contract, both parties must offer reasonable consideration.*

As I mentioned in the "Tale of a Hundred Knights," when you make loans out of thin air, there is no way to pay the interest back because there is not enough money created to cover the interest and the bank does not offer any consideration for the loan other than the paper and ink the loan agreement is printed on. There have been court cases that support this legal truth (7). So if the bank makes a

---

[3]  03/06/2009 by Thomas Kostigen title *"The 700 Trillion Elephant"* (http://www.marketwatch.com/story/the-700-trillion-elephant-room-theres)

bad deal, it's the banks fault, not ours. They should have invented a system wherein they would actually get paid.

That being said, one has to realize the whole financial system of the world is built on this larceny.

*How can we change the system without disrupting and destroying everything we have?*

What is clear is that fresh money is required by the economic systems in operation now. We hear about quantitative easing in the financial news. This is just a fancy term for hyperinflation of the money supply (2). This is good and proves my point that fresh money is essential to the economy. However, new currency created by new debt is bad and unfeasible because it just perpetuates the system of diminishing returns while the incurable debt and the bank's claim of ownership grows exponentially.

> If all the debt is paid off, won't everything stop?
>
> I answer this question by saying, "Will you ever stop getting hungry? Will you stop needing new clothes or repairs to your house? Then how can everything stop?" In the NPCB model, demand will be the driving force. You will no longer have the threat of being homeless, and joblessness won't matter. You will be provided funds for extra safety as a surplus or savings or for consumption of goods and services. Don't fear getting ahead and being prosperous.

There are a few things that people will always need. According to Maslow's hierarchy of needs (14), the basic needs are food, water, shelter, and love. These things will always be in demand. Everyone will need fresh food, fresh water, clean and sound shelter, and love. Everything else is not needed, and wise people do not spend money on things they do not need.

*Using credit cards to fulfill one's basic needs is a worst-case scenario.*

A vibrant economy is dependent upon not saving money but spending it all on stuff. The advertising for this is very powerful and sustains a sense of insecurity in your mind that motivates you to collect needless stuff that will become trash in less than six months. This is not because of the law of supply and demand; rather it is the rule of "move as much crap as you can" and the ability to buy that feeds the debt-ownership machine.

"Move as much crap as you can" means that all products must move. Move from the producer to the store, to the consumer, then to the trash heap. For business to stay in business, they have to always sell products, even if everyone already has one. So they carefully design everything to fall apart at a time when you would go and buy another one rather than do without. Additionally, they stop supporting old computer operating systems so you always have to purchase a new device.

What makes this possible is credit. Credit is the rain to the parched desert of personal finance. Ever wonder why your bills are due on a calendar date like the first or the fifteenth and you're paid on a weekday like every other Wednesday or Friday? Because those times will not line up at several times during the year; *this means* banks and merchants whom you owe can charge you extra fees for late payments and overdrafts.

It was rumored in 2014 that banks collected $30 billion in overdraft fees (20). They took $30 billion from people who have no money. Banks love this.

*Enter the credit card.*

The credit card is fresh money when you need some. You can spend up to the limit and take fifteen years to pay it off, if ever. If you have overdraft protection on your checking account, it means they will use your savings account as a credit card to cover your checking balance.

Credit cards increase the general public's ability to buy. This is the lifeblood of the American economy. Without credit, there will be days when you can't go and buy something—no fast food, no pay per view, no coffee, nothing until you get paid again and your paycheck clears.

The economy runs on a constant supply of new currency, in the form of credit card debt, to purchase needless products made by slave labor in what we label developing nations. Business stays open by moving needless products through the doors via credit and government subsidy (21). Credit is the primary operating principle in today's economy. Credit provides ability to buy. Without credit, the only ability to buy would come from savings, and savings are the primary target of the economic roller coaster.

# CHAPTER 4

# Profit

*Profit* is the accounting term for the amount of money left over from sales of goods and services after business operating costs are subtracted. Profit is what every business, every corporation, and every bank in the world is working for. Profit is the primary motivation for capitalism. The goal of capitalism is being able to collect enough currency to pay for your desired lifestyle for the rest of your life and the life of your lineage. Corporations exist for profit at all costs. Profit is not necessarily beneficial to the individual or the environment. There are two types of profit that I have observed—what I call micro profit and macro profit.

## Microprofit

Microprofit is what the individual strives for through small business and investing. Most successful businesses go through a time of rapid growth and then plateau. They then try to maintain this plateau of profitability, because profit is synonymous with growth. A company is considered a good company if it can maintain a 15 or 20 percent profit margin consistently. All our retirement plans are dependent on stock market microprofits. Buying low and selling high is the microprofit strategy. Microprofits are used to spur the economy through consumption of goods and services and to provide funding for costs of living as well as supplemental luxuries, education, travel, and personal pursuits and interests.

Your 401(k), SEPP, and Roth IRAs are all funded by microprofits, stored with the hopes of even more growth. This growth depends on yet more microprofits from other business investments. Microprofits are the realm of the larger economy that is used to facilitate happiness for all.

## Macroprofit

Macroprofit is the main goal of large industry: gasoline, oil, electrical power, pharmaceuticals, banking, communication, information technology, military industrial complex, aerospace, and any other large industry with government subsidy and involvement. They consistently maintain large profit margins well above 500 percent.

Macroprofits are detrimental to the economy. That is because the massive amounts of currency taken out of circulation by macroprofits drain the populace of consumption power. Remember, a vibrant economy is dependent not on saving money but spending it all on stuff. *This necessitates a constant supply of fresh money in order for any economy to function.* Employees of macroprofit industries and governments do not benefit beyond compensation for labor and some benefits.

Macroprofit motives destroy the environment, create and sustain war, inhibit education and development of new technologies outside the existing enclave, create toxic waste, create toxic products, and facilitate the decline of health of people and the extinction of plants and animals. Large corporate bonuses are derived from macroprofits.

*Most of the beneficial goods and services needed to maintain a happy, healthy, and clean society are not profitable businesses.*

Health care, infrastructure development and maintenance, education, and environmental clean-up and protection, preservation, and conservation are just a few examples of vital and essential sectors for sustainability that wither because they are not profitable—totally beneficial, but not profitable. So states and municipalities fund these essential yet unprofitable sectors with bonds and revenue from parking tickets and the like, which we all appreciate so much.

CHAPTER 5

# Wages

Wages are compensation for labor (money for work, a.k.a. earnings). Wages are what the average person uses to live on and what the economy depends on as the primary source of funds for consumption. *Everything in the economy depends on the individual's ability to consume.* Therefore, the economy is mostly dependent on wages. Larger wages enable vigorous and widespread consumption. Vigorous consumption far and wide means a thriving economy. A thriving economy means everyone is enjoying more happiness.

## Disposable Wages

*Disposable wages* is the term for the amount of money earned from labor that is not spent on living expenses. This money is wisely saved for retirement and a targeted resource by credit lenders. The advertisers create a poor self-image in your mind and then motivate you to buy something new, something big. The lenders use a ratio of debt (*cost of living*) to income (*wages*) to determine how much disposable wages are available for debt repayment, and they'll tailor their credit cards and home and auto loans to absorb every dollar not otherwise accounted for.

## Income

Income is microprofit derived from investing wages (money from money). The word *income* has slowly been corrupted to include wages. In this way, the macroprofit elements of the banking industry can seize or tax your labor. If they can tax your labor, you are working for free and are therefore a slave with illusions of freedom and delusions of choice. The extent to which your wages are taxed as income is the extent to which you are working for free (enslaved).[4]

## Disposable Income

Disposable income is similar to disposable wages. Disposable income is the amount of income/wages you do not spend on your cost of living or have tied up in investments, a.k.a. liquid assets or cash; it is actually unspent wages for most people, best used for saving and investments. To be considered real disposable income, it has to come from unpurposed microprofits that you don't mind spending willy-nilly on fun or gambling. You get disposable income from investing your wages. Disposable income is what the banks and finance companies use to determine how much money they can lend you. The more disposable income you have, the larger the loan you can qualify for. The loan is limited by the amount of disposable monthly income (wages for most people) available for monthly loan repayments.

---

[4]  1883: *Butchers' Union Co. v. Crescent City Co., 111 U.S. 746* defines *labor* as property—and the most sacred kind of property. "Among these unalienable rights, as proclaimed in the Declaration of Independence is the right of men to pursue their happiness, by which is meant, the right any lawful business or vocation, in any manner not inconsistent with the equal rights of others, which may increase their prosperity or develop their faculties, so as to give them their highest enjoyment . . . It has been well said that '*the property which every man has is his own labor, as it is the original foundation of all other property so it is the most sacred and inviolable*'" (emphasis mine).

CHAPTER 6

# Cost of Living

The cost of living is the amount of money required to pay for the basic and essential necessities of healthy life. These costs of living include food, water, shelter, clothing, gas, electric, communication, and transportation. Most people have to pay for these necessities solely from their wages; their wages are being taxed as income.

*They consider everything beyond basic necessities a luxury or a privilege.* As our technological world advances, it drags with it the requirement for more necessary costs for modern living—for instance, computers. Now almost all government services are avoiding personal interaction in favor of Internet-only service. So now it has become a requirement to have a computer in order to use government services. What used to take a phone call now requires a computer—not only a computer, but Internet access as well. And the software upgrades constantly, so you have to purchase new machines with higher, more expensive Internet speeds and computer hardware. Figure in the frequency at which the computers need upgrading, and it becomes a serious increase in your cost of living.

If the cost of living exceeds wages, then an oppressive economic climate is established, requiring additional credit to make up the difference.

# CHAPTER 7

# Manufacturing

Businesses that sell products they manufacture are dependent on two things to remain profitable and therefore sustainable. They require large profit margins and never-ending demand for their products.

*The biggest threat to profit margins is employee wages and benefits* (22).

Business, being self-centered by design, thinks only of itself as disconnected from the rest of society. Paranoid of competition, ruthless, and greedy, business will do anything that it can to increase its own profits. It considers only its product and market to further profits.

*The cost of production is the largest obstacle to macroprofits for business.* They do not consider that their employees are firstly consumers and therefore also their customers. By moving manufacturing to cheap foreign labor (slaves), they unknowingly alienate their consumer market (22). The consumer market is the people they no longer employ because their jobs have been moved, so they no longer have the means to purchase their company's products.

Business then becomes reliant on the banks to provide consumers with the power to purchase their products in the form of credit (debt). This is not a sustainable business condition. As the consumer base already has barely enough power to consume the basics of living, it is only a matter of time before the consumer base cannot pay the interest on the credit required. At that point, the bank, business, and the family collapse from poor financial structure.

For the business that manages to continue to manufacture domestically, there is a constant attempt to pay their employees less and less, withhold benefits, and resist the labor forces' attempts to unionize. Business sees all these as threats to its own psychotic, selfish profit potential.

The reality is that a small fraction of consumers (employees) are fighting for a stronger ability to consume. Higher wages means higher consumption ability, which also means more units will be consumed, which means more profits over time. This is also known as *sustainability*. The ability of the market to consume products and services is dependent on the consumer having disposable income/wages to purchase manufactured products without relying on debt (credit).

# CHAPTER 8

# Pricing

Pricing has always boggled my mind until I saw a great film called *The Story of Stuff* (23). In this twenty-minute film, they show how things can be made, imported, and sold at or below cost of manufacture, externalizing the costs of labor by using economic slaves in the Third World to make a technical item like an alarm clock cheaper to produce than a fast food meal. It becomes cheaper for the consumer and yet more profitable for the producer. Does this sound too good to be true? It is true, and the karmic cost in human and environmental suffering for these economic shortcuts may exact a terrible price.

## Pricing Is the Throttle of the Economy

If prices are low, then products move rapidly, and the economy booms. There is no better example of this than Black Friday. On this day, the entire retail industry competes to have the lowest possible prices. This gets frenzied consumers to line up in the early morning darkness to acquire otherwise unobtainable electronics, furniture, holiday gifts, etc. Many of the products sold are priced so below cost it is inconceivable to me that this is considered "in the black" or profitable. I have heard that many retail businesses depend on the volume of Black Friday to establish their entire profits for the year and remain open.

The question is, if most of the items are sold at below cost, *how is it profitable*? The answer must lie in how they look at it. If they move certain high-demand items below cost to attract consumers, then do they rely on the volume of customers already in the store to move other regularly priced or marked-up items to make up the difference? In any case, the fact is the same; *low prices move items and accelerate consumption*. This is due to the fact that wages are stagnant, so any opportunity for the consumer to purchase otherwise unaffordable items must be utilized. The economy booms on Black Friday. If the entire year of retail sales depends on this day, then imagine all the days with the same low prices.

## Do High Prices Serve the Economy?

Furthermore, prices are commonly associated with inflation. When prices go up, they call that inflation as well. This is known as the inflation rate and is identified by a general rise in prices and stated as a percentage, not an increase in the money supply. To raise prices is completely contrary to the ideal that movement of inventory through retail business is the heartbeat of a good economy. If the example of Black Friday is valid, when there is a surplus of disposable wages or available credit, it would stand to reason that *lower prices* would be the way to go to move the economy onward and boost retailers' profits. Raising prices because people have more implied purchasing power inhibits consumption. They will just save their money and wait for a sale.

The big money players point to other factors for higher prices. Higher wholesale or shipping costs are the first factors that come to mind. Then there are also arguments about demand, political encumbrances, price fixing, and just plain old greed.

Of course, it could all just be razzle-dazzle and make-believe. If the media tells you that selling millions of items below cost is somehow profitable, most of us just shrug and make-believe they understand it. It would take a massive audit to bring the truth to light. If selling below cost is profitable, then it must be the *invisible hand* that makes up the difference for the retailer. Why can't the *invisible hand* do the same for consumers?

## How Much Is Enough?

There are plenty of rules of thumb for profits, such as the 300 percent mark-up, the 500 percent, and even the over 900 percent in the case of gas pump prices and more than 1,200 percent plus in pharmaceuticals. One would think with all this macroprofit taking in the big sectors, like energy and pharmaceuticals, there would be more competition regulating prices. Competition, that thing they assured us in economy class, would regulate the market and pricing and maintain the balance between cost of living and wages.

It is clearly evident that price fixing is the norm and the cost of living is way out of balance with wages. As I have stated earlier, *if the cost of living exceeds wages, then debt is required to make up the difference*. As we all know, debt is time in servitude or slavery, and the bank owns all of it.

The focus of pricing is misplaced on the quarterly measure of success of the business. The focus of pricing must be to favor the greater good of the economy (i.e., the longevity of the business). There will always be a gap between market price, wholesale price, retail price, and the consumers' ability to pay.

Prices are not directly related to the volume of money available in circulation. Prices are just need versus greed, pure and simple. If prices are not controlled by market competition or government regulation, then the desire for profit by business will raise prices, which will create an oppressive economy, where the cost of living far exceeds wages.

The government affects sticker prices by paying the difference in various ways. The most important would be subsidizing (giving money debt-free) to the companies it has been paid to favor. They also increase or decrease import tariffs on products to play favorites and limit competition. If the proper lobbyist pays the correct senator, then the import tariff disappears, and/or taxpayer subsidies repay the investment exponentially (24). If not, then a tariff is collected, and that importer's product price is no longer competitive. Why is there only one company that is allowed to import sugar into the United States? It also happens to be the most expensive sugar in the world.

## Price Fixing

Price fixing is when a monopoly is charging oppressive prices for necessary goods and services to the people and when all the companies that provide the same goods or service agree to charge excessively high prices to extort exaggerated profits.

The privatization of water is a perfect example. There are other ways to fix prices besides backroom deals. "Industry standards" are price fixing in disguise. If retailers cannot agree on prices for retail items legally, then they agree to charge the consumer extra charges like restocking fees.

When I was working for a large, well-known, venerable retail chain that prided itself on customer service, they started to arbitrarily charge restocking fees. I knew this would alienate our customers. When I asked why we were abandoning our good policy of returns with no questions asked in favor of 30 percent restocking fees, my manager's response was "Because everyone else is doing it." We lost half of our customers . . .

Retailers are very creative in inventing new terminology to charge frivolous fees that make up the difference between what they want to charge for a product and what they have to charge within the law (examples like restocking fees, store credit, and service charges). These fees, not being tied to any product but instead tied to store policy, are being applied to all consumers patronizing the store. It is very nice padding for their profit margins at the cost of customer satisfaction, customer service, and consumer confidence. If all the similar companies are using the same "standard" and the consumer has no choice but to pay, then this is a veiled price fix that is largely ignored by government and resented by the consumer. This results in an unnecessarily exaggerated cost of living at the expense of the greater economic health in the name of profit.

# CHAPTER 9

# Business

On one hand, business is a family tradition, a life's work, a vehicle for prosperity, a community icon, a reason to get up and get going. On the other, it is an accounting game and a ruthless and impersonal power trip. Business exists to create products and services for the "market"—or people in actuality.

In order for business to remain open, they have to generate enough profit to pay wages and benefits to its employees and provide reinvestment capital and debt repayment as well as a standard of living desirable to the owner/creator of the business. Unfortunately, it has become modern business policy to cut employee wages and benefits to redistribute those funds to personal profits of the company officers as bonuses.

Business is a great way to spend one's life for the passion of doing, creating, and accomplishing. Identifying a need and filling it or supplying the remedy to satisfy that need is rewarding and fulfilling. When created for the soul of the owner and the customer as a person, business is a noble and valuable use of the precious time we are given here in life.

Because of the mind-numbing and soul-crushing financial game, business is also a torment sent straight from the bowels of hell. The modern financial landscape that business must survive in is toxic and barren of spiritual reward. Without a huge reserve of operating capital, most businesses do not survive infancy. It is widely known that most businesses lose money for the first five years. So at least five years of operating capital in reserve is ideal.

Banks know this but don't support new businesses through the vulnerable stages of building a customer base, building up sales receipts, and so on. If a business were a baby infant and the bank its parents, the bank would supply one diaper and two bottles of milk. After that, the infant would be "on its own" and expected to pay its own way without complaint.

A business plan is created to show the bank how much money the business will make. It identifies the market, the product or service, and the design and the scope of the business. It shows how much the business will cost to run and how much more than that it can "reasonably" take in. The passion of the soul is forsaken because it is not quantifiable and therefore irrelevant in the cold hell of the finance. *Remember, nothing beneficial is profitable—i.e., health care, social services and education, or spiritual satisfaction.*

Business does not want to pay employees but has to by law. It creates a wide and varying spectrum of wages paid, depending on the geographical location of the labor. Business wants to charge as much as possible for its products to maximize profits. The biggest expenditure of business is employee wages and benefits (22). This explains why there is such a strong resistance to organized labor unions that will fix high wages and benefits for all workers.

Businesses that provide goods or services that people do not actually need in their lives have to advertise the hardest. They have to recognize the consumers in the market/community that might buy their products and services if they could. This is why they try to artificially create a larger market share by using manipulative psychological advertising and manipulate public opinion of their products and services through mass media "buzz" (15). *If it's advertised on TV, you probably don't need it.* On the other hand, a business that provides products and services that people actually need—like groceries, medical care, medicine, and energy—can charge as much as they want, and people will have to pay.

Businesses that provide products and services that people actually need are often deeply ingrained in the government that historically is supposed to regulate them by breaking up both monopolies and trusts and prohibiting illegal price fixing. If these businesses charge as much as they want for basic necessities, like water or pharmaceuticals, they will eventually oppress the community/market and extort power and influence beyond the role of a mere business. That is why there are so many laws on the books to prevent this and the resultant suffering of the people.

*Business itself is not sustainable.*

Business is vulnerable to myriad variables in the economic and physical environment. Technology changes, resources dry up, consumer capacity and/or demand ebbs and flows to reveal the mortal life of a business. Most businesses are developed solely to create an income stream for the people who collect the profits (as per the economic principle that all activities in the market are for a self-serving interest). There are no limits to the type and character of a business. If it does prove to have some relative longevity in the market/community, then at the time of the owners' retirement or death, the small business is usually sold or closed.

It seems irresponsible to me for the government to favor business health in financial terms above the overall financial health of the economy and the physical health of the populace, the consumers.

# CHAPTER 10

# Loans

When something is loaned from one person to another, the person loaning goes without the use but still maintains ownership. The borrower has use of the item temporarily and promises to return the item in good condition, presumably. Without the agreement to return, it is a gift or a theft, and ownership is forfeit or transferred, depending on how you want to look at it.

Money, a medium for exchange, is created by agreement among the people. When money is loaned, the agreement is between the lender and the borrower. The lender supplies only the amount needed by the borrower, which is called principal. The borrower has to agree to return or repay the amount borrowed (principal) plus the microprofit for the lender, commonly known as interest.

When a business, like a bank, loans money to an individual or another business, it creates the money with a promise to repay (loan contract). The borrower then has a schedule to repay the amount loaned (principal) plus extra microprofit (interest). The loan principal is created as new currency. The interest exists only as an idea. Rather than use existing money owned by the bank (profits), the bank just creates new money with limits based on a percentage of total deposits. The principal is a fixed amount, static. However, the interest is eternal and grows exponentially with capitalization (interest charged on interest).

The bank is interested in the transaction because of the potential for profit or ownership of the fruit of labor of the person or business borrowing the money. If the borrower cannot pay the interest fee on the loan, the bank seizes ownership of the product (collateral) created from the principal provided. This can be buildings, machines, products, stocks, or more money possessed elsewhere by the borrower.

When one borrows from the bank, one is selling whatever it is the loan is for to the bank with the hopes of buying it back. This applies to all loans—from private loans between people to nations borrowing from the World Bank.

# CHAPTER 11

# Government

*"Of the people, by the people, for the people."*

The government is composed of people—people like you and me, who also suffer under the corrupt banking system and fear debt, poverty, and destitution. Because they fear being poor, they use their positions in government foremost to gain personal wealth instead of to serve the interests of the poor and downtrodden, the very ones who need their best interests protected. These poor people are the ones who presumably cast their votes and trusted the candidate to protect their rights and interests.

The government of the United States has become privatized by corporate and banking interests and derelict in its duty to the *people*. It has basically sold the value of the people's labor in the form of bonds attached to birth certificates to be used as collateral to inflate the money supply via debt (7).

This favors only the central bank and is of no benefit to the people. The central bank then shares these bonds with corporations that invest them in the stock market for corporate benefit and profit. The people whose lives have been monetized (labor sold) by these bonds will never see a dime of the profits their bonded labor yields.

Government uses public money to pay subsidies to corporations that monopolize markets, pay subpoverty wages, and wage real wars for fictitious reasons. They basically sell the judicial and political power of their seats to lobbyists for private corporate interests through obscene campaign funding like super-PACs. In spite of whatever they promised the people who actually voted for them, they write and support legislation that permits destruction of the natural environment, corrupts the food supply, and forces the impoverished to pay for services they might not otherwise need if they already had nutritious food and stable, warm housing—all while the politicians enjoy collecting middleman fees, like commissions and stock. The purpose of representative government is to protect the interests of the weakest and most vulnerable in society, not to prey on them for profit.

Government has stopped serving the poor and middle class and seeks to serve the profit-minded corporations instead.

The corporation is immortal, immune to accountability and responsibility, and has no national loyalty other than the position that yields the most profit. Corporations hold no allegiance higher than to that of profit. They will destroy anything that gets in the way of their profits. It is the principal corruptor of the government, and its primary power source is money.

CHAPTER 12

# Health Care

Health care is a simple problem. From its inception, the AMA has been a subordinate entity to the pharmaceutical industry (25). The entire education and practice of medicine has been to focus treatment on illness and disease with prescription medications. So far, there have been some good advances with antibiotics and vaccines curing numerous diseases of devastating pathology.

Of course, as nature finds a way, these treatments are arguably becoming more harmful than beneficial. With widespread use of antibiotics, the bacteria are adapting to resist the medicines that used to cure bacterial infections. Vaccines, created to stop viral epidemics, now cause autism, ADHD, and generally degrade the health of the individual (26) (27).

So what are doctors to do? They have been taught all their lives that antibiotics treat infections, but now they are *causing* unstoppable infections. Viral diseases (like VRE, MRSA) are being traded for mild brain damage, and the big pharma is now happily producing both vaccines and the medications for the symptoms of vaccine-induced brain damage—all at a huge profit. Most recently, the federal government has determined that everyone *will* need a doctor so they are forcing everyone to buy private health insurance (Affordable Care

Act). Private public health insurance by federal mandate seems unfair and a clear indicator of corruption.

*Health care is beneficial, not profitable.*

The most afflicted are the least able to pay for such service. The huge cost of medical supplies, strong demand for high salaries by doctors and nurses in the US, and expensive malpractice insurance weigh the scale heavily toward cost of operation outmatching the payments received by the poor or infirm.

Health insurance companies, like HMOs, available only to those who are employed, are a compromise. The doctors and clinics are contracted and receive a monthly fee for every member enrolled with their group. This is a great deal as long as the majority of the members ever need care. This is because the monthly payment to the HMO per member is lower than the provider cost of a single clinic visit. They make up for it by efficient organization and aggressive treatment protocols. The clinics use call centers to handle as many patient concerns over the phone as they can. General health questions, prescription refills, and triage are handled by the call center. This is to keep them from visiting the clinic if it is not medically necessary. When they do have to come in to actually see the doctor, they see a nurse practitioner or physician's assistant more often than not. The NPs and PAs do a great job and handle the most common causes of clinic visits with superb expertise. They free up the MDs to focus on more complex cases. All the treatments are aggressive, and the patient is cured in the shortest amount of time, so they won't need to visit the clinic very often.

*The cost of the health care business is out of balance.*

Hospitals are a necessary service for a modern civilization. It is a business model doomed to failure. Doctors, administrators, nurses, and medical equipment manufacturers all want the big money lifestyle while serving a population with little or no disposable income. In other words, the patients who need health care the most do not have enough money to give the health care provider. If you have an HMO, your clinic will share the cost of your hospitalization with your insurance company. This is the conflict of interest that gave HMOs a bad rep. Both the insurance company and the HMO are motivated to take shortcuts with your care to keep their costs low. The more these companies focused being profitable instead of providing a necessary service responsibly, the more they began to deny services. They fell into the "not my problem" attitude about "pre-existing conditions" and denied payment or treatment that eventually came to include life-saving procedures and diagnostic studies. They threw the baby out with the bath water.

The profit centric businesses that used to pay for their employees' health insurance are choosing to pocket those benefit payments instead. Insurance companies rely on volume in order to stay in business. They require more healthy people paying into the system without using the benefits that generate payouts. Often, when members do require high-cost services, the insurance company will deny authorization to treat and/or refuse to pay after the fact.

*High cost services are beneficial, not profitable.*

This is the Obama care debacle. It has created a national HMO, and everyone, working or not, has to pay into this. This is doomed to failure because as the population ages, people will need more and more high-cost care. The GMO food supply is keeping people sick, in need of care, and unable to work. The vaccination schedules are creating a generation afflicted with various forms of autism and weak immune systems, which will need medication in order to function. Of course, the only way Obamacare can function as a for-profit business is to cut services and staff and raise prices.

Once again, we see the self-destructive corporate model engineering a system failure. The employers don't want a lot of staff to pay and do not want to pay the staff a lot. Therefore, the staff, overworked and underpaid, cannot afford to pay for insurance or medical services, but now they have to even if they are healthy.

Money is the crux of the problem. The health care debacle is perpetuated by the constant flood of toxins and carcinogens into the food supply and environment in the name of profit. These toxins in the food supply cause illness and disease throughout the population and will overwhelm a privatized, profit-oriented health system that wants to keep staff and services to a minimum and charges high prices.

Mental health care is ignored and absent from covered benefits because it is so subjective in nature. There is no way for a corporate accountant with a medical terminology book to write a specific treatment protocol that says your depression and anxiety will be cured in ten visits with a therapist. It is of epidemic proportions, and it is much easier to ignore the existence of this huge problem rather than deal with it and expose the root cause, modern technological society.

One way to ease the pressure on health care is to have a healthy population that does not need medical services often. Prevention is worth a pound of cure. A natural food supply, clean environment, and plenty of exercise are all that are needed to stay healthy. The reality is, the government-subsidized food industry produces enormous amounts of food that are full of toxins, chemicals, GMO ingredients, hormones, and antibiotics because they profit from them. All these toxins cause illness and disease over time. Other profit-driven companies lobby the government to be permitted to increase pollution levels to make their production cheaper. A polluted environment causes illness and disease. Because everyone has to work most of the day, most of the people live a sedentary lifestyle. They sit at work, they sit at home, and they sit when they drive around. Lack of exercise causes illness and disease. Very few of us actually decide to eat crap, breathe crap, and sit around a chemical dump. The choices are very limited.

# CHAPTER 13

# Education

Educational system is a problem because it is not educating the children. Every generation of children is becoming more and more autistic from forced vaccination schedules, pesticides, and genetically modified processed food. Autism is a spectrum of learning disorders with many levels to include a big-pharma favorite, ADHD.

It is obvious to me that the powers that be know this and are buckling down by changing the educational system from intellectual development to a reform school environment of conformity and obedience. The quality of information being offered is falling ever lower and lower on the priority list in favor of stricter clothing regulation, thought control, behavior modification, and now religious indoctrination.

The children are not being taught to think but rather to memorize and repeat phrases and tasks. This is probably due to the now majority of learning disabled, medicated students in class. The medical industry causes brain damage with vaccines, vaccines are required to attend school, all children must attend school. See the no-win situation for the average child?

Higher education is in swift decline in the United States. Every year they seem to lower the SAT requirement and raise tuition. And still, I see the media deterring beneficial intellectual majors in favor of more "employable" majors. It is my opinion that higher education is for personal fulfillment, not vocational training.

In higher education, people can cluster in closed societies like fraternities and sororities. The culture of the Greek system extents beyond university campuses to all the rest of the professional clubs, like the AMA, the Bar, the National Association of Realtors. All these are private clubs that control various public resources and services.

With future generations poised to remain ever more learning disabled, indoctrinated, and obedient, the industrial military complex will have a good supply of fodder for the perpetual global wars for profit.

# CHAPTER 14

# War

War is being used to control resources, trade, and development of emerging markets. You will not be willing to invest your money for anything in a war zone. Neither will anyone else. If you cannot invest in an area, war in that area is good way to make sure no one else does either (28) (29).

*When they say, "In the interest of free trade," what they mean is for the interest of a global trade monopoly.*

# CHAPTER 15

# Housing

The problem with housing is the fact that real estate is the method by which banks and the nation derive their value. Real estate is regarded as an investment, and there are many investors who buy low and sell high. Real estate is also traded on the stock exchanges and by collections of investors pooling their monies together in real estate investment trusts (REITs) and "mortgage-backed securities." There are real estate development companies as well as real estate financing companies that are also publically traded.

Real estate is coarsely divided into sections depending on use like residential, commercial, and agricultural. Every level of government has these uses for land mapped out in zones. This zone, that zone, and mixed-use zones all have special codes and jargon.

Real estate is a good investment if it goes up in value from the time you buy it to the time you sell it. Income property is land and buildings you let others use and collect rent. Ideally, the amount of rent you collect is more than the loan repayment and taxes and fees associated with ownership of the land and buildings. This may also be a good investment if you collect more than you spend. This is confusing to me because real estate buildings begin to decay almost as soon as they are constructed. Weather, insects, rot, fire, and vandalism all destroy the building on the land and therefore the value should reflect that.

This is where the inspector comes in. He or she is supposed to have some sort of knowledge of construction and local building codes. The inspector crawls around to measure the degree of degeneration a building being considered for sale has endured and give a reliable assessment of its value. Unfortunately, this is not actually reliable, as there is no particular requirement to become a building inspector nor is there any responsibility held by the building inspectors if they miss big or little deficiencies in the building's integrity. Most often, the opinion they give favors the position of the body who hires them. For example, if the seller of a building hires the inspector, most often there will be nothing wrong with the building on the report, regardless of the actual condition of the property. If the buyer hires the inspector, depending on the desired amount of leverage, things will be seen that aren't actually there; they will report rooms smaller than they actually are or falsely find nothing wrong at all in order to grease the wheels so the deal can go through.

The banks will use these inspection reports to approve or deny loan applications or adjust loan amounts. This is great if the inspection is professional and impartial and conducted by competent inspectors. It can really be an accurate appraisal of the value of the property on the table. Unfortunately, this is frequently not the case. Inspections are opinions for hire and rarely reflect reality. This creates an environment where the value of a property becomes very subjective. It shifts and moves like sand. As the financial foundation of the nation, real estate value should not shift like sand.

## Valuation

As real estate is the measure of value used by the nation and the banks, the measure of how real estate is valued becomes crucial. Real estate value is measured in several ways:

1. *Cost of new construction.* This is materials + labor = cost/value.

2. *Cost of replacement.* If a particular artistry was used in the original construction, the current cost of similar artisans and exotic materials are estimated again as materials + labor = cost or value.
3. *Comparable valuation.* "How much did someone else pay for a similarly sized house and lot nearby? Then that's what this one is worth." Unfortunately, the comparable means of valuation is the most common because it provides the greatest potential for volatility and hopefully equity growth, a.k.a. profit. For income property, the amount of rents collected is the means of valuation.

Comparable valuation is the worst means of a keystone valuation because it easily strays far from reality. Since 1999, the banking regulations for real estate loans and who can issue these loans were cast aside by President Clinton (30). That started the real estate "bubble," during which real estate prices quadrupled in as many years, using comparable valuation. During this bubble, the banks would make outrageous deals. In order to make the debt-to-income ratio conform, they would offer US$700,000 to a borrower with no job, income, or assets (ninja loan) at 0.05 percent interest and require interest-only payments for the first five years of a thirty- or forty- or fifty-year mortgage. The banks used the inflated mortgages as securities and borrowed from themselves twenty to thirty times the value of all the mortgages in that time (18). They displayed the currency they created by lending left hand to the right hand of the bank as profits from these secretly toxic securities and sold them across the world. It was a big long money con.

Another mechanism that enables the banks to make unrealistic loans to consumers is the ability to resell the loan. The bank protects itself from loss by selling the debt contract at face value to the government (similar to money laundering). Before the ink is dry, mortgage loans are resold to the government agencies known as Federal National Mortgage Association (FNMA), commonly known as Fannie Mae, and Federal Home Loan Mortgage Corporation (FHLMC), known as Freddie Mac, if they conform. The borrower must have a certain debt-to-income ratio for the loan to be resold (hence, the small fraction of interest charge and initial interest-only payments divided over longer time periods, to keep the payments low). Loans that meet these requirements are known as conforming loans and are eligible to be purchased by the government. Before 1999, these government agencies looked at the entire life of the loan to determine if it was conforming or not. After 1999, they just looked at the debt-to-income ratios of the first day of the loan. The results were disastrous for people and nations.

This had terrible ramifications that echoed across the world. As well we all should know, in the real estate collapse of 2006, realized in 2008, FNMA and FHLMC both failed as well as the largest company that insured everything, AIG.

This would not have happened if valuation of real estate was based on cost of new construction or cost of replacement for conforming loans. With pricing anchored to labor and materials, the prices would not be able to inflate so quickly. Instead of a bubble, there would be a tide.

# CHAPTER 16

# The Justice System

The problem with the justice system is that it too has been privatized by exclusive clubs and corporations. Corporations have purchased most of the judges on the Supreme Court, the appellate courts, and the lower courts. Several judges on the Supreme Court were once corporate lawyers and still judge cases clearly against the ideals of constitution and in support of the corporate agenda of disempowerment of the people and to coerce labor.

This is easily done because the entire system is privatized by a club known as the Bar. You will not be allowed to deal in court without belonging to this club. It is the deal that is the real insult to justice. Since all sides belong to this club, the defendants are usually outsiders. Their fates are negotiated and traded like baseball card instead of people. These people are urged to do what they are told with regard to plea bargains, bench deals, etc., often for the convenience of the system rather than to serve justice. This bastardizes justice by changing the charges, or conditions, in order to convenience the club members. For example, I was in traffic court and watched people fight parking tickets. They had photos and valid cases for the most part, and the club member judge would give them all the same option: "Plead guilty, and I will suspend the fine." None of them were guilty. The judge was hiding the number of bad tickets to boost revenue for the city. It is not just to ask an innocent person to plead guilty in return for no punishment when no punishment is warranted, as they were innocent in the first place. The private clubs make a mockery out of justice.

*People or corporations that have deep pockets have an unfair advantage in the court system.*

An unfair advantage is not good for the country or the world while it hangs over an environmental precipice. A person or corporation has the advantage and can press an unjust or even unlawful position, using threats of poverty against their opposition. Take Thomas Edison versus George Westinghouse for control of the electronic industry in the United States. The two entrepreneurs engaged in a competition to determine what would be the dominant electrical system in the United States. Thomas Edison built the first generator and wired John Rockefeller's house with electricity with the intent to sell it as superior to kerosene lamp lighting. He used direct current, or DC. It was George Westinghouse together with Nicolai Tesla who developed alternating current and built the first hydroelectric power plant at Niagara Falls and won the "war of the currents." Embittered by his loss and with much deeper pockets, Edison forced Westinghouse to sell him all his electrical patents or be ruined and impoverished by threat of long, costly, perpetual lawsuits and court proceedings. Edison then took Westinghouse's and Tesla's patents and founded General Electric (25).

*If you built it, it should be yours.*

No one should be able to take what is yours away from you in a court of law simply because they have more currency than you. Imagine how your life would be different if you didn't have to pay out of your pocket for private legal matters.

The destruction of the middle class financially has added to this one-sided legal tyranny. With a vibrant and attentive middle class, a just cause could rally enough funding to challenge large corporations in just courts. Hence, it has been systematically gutted.

*Whistle blowing, once the job of the police department, has now been criminalized.*

Those good people of conscience who expose wrongdoings are regarded as criminals and punished with harassment, prosecution, and jail (Julian Assange, Edward Snowden). The judges rule in favor of the corporations over and over again. They are no longer impartial or ethical in the practice of law.

Whistle-blowing is a primary function of the first amendment, free speech. If there was ever something to speak up about, corruption and criminality are of highest public concern. If a person cannot speak up without fear of prosecution, then there is no free speech.

Secondly, the justice system is currently in the process of actually being privatized by corporations. Right now, you can build a prison, hire private staff, and contract it out to the state for custodianship of the convicted. This is compounded by conflict of interest when judges and attorneys are shareholders in the prison-for-profit system. There have been several cases where judges were caught sending people to the prison they own willy-nilly to boost their personal profits.

A perfect example of the justice system being manipulated for private gain is juvenile court. Juvenile court is in a realm between jurisdictions, and there is no clear place for juveniles to stand legally. The fate of the juvenile in the court system is completely held in the hands of the social workers. Every day you hear about juveniles being arrested for ridiculous reasons, going to court and ending up in some private, state-funded "boot camp" from which they never seem to improve enough to be released. All the while, the company running the camp gets a fat paycheck from the state.

*Law enforcement has become corrupted in its own right.*

Across the nation, police departments protect unlawful behavior with a code of silence. Police kill innocent people, often with impunity. They blatantly lie in reports and on the stand to protect one another from prosecution.

The courts favor the word of a police officer above common sense or good reason because they are club members. If you try to make a complaint about an individual police officer, you are confronted, threatened, harassed, arrested, or even killed in the USA.

Extrajudicial punishment administered by police has become the standard for law enforcement practice in the United States. Good sense will tell you that extrajudicial punishment is pure vigilantism. Vigilantism is bad because innocent individuals are often targeted for convenience, being at the wrong place at the wrong time, rather than being protected through the due process of law.

*Law is nothing without due process.*

Every time the police abandon due process and administer punishment to anyone, guilty or not, they are in violation of the law and derelict of their duty. They should be fired. It is not the job of law enforcement to administer punishment. It is the duty of the court to administer fair and just punishment under the law. This is what rule of law is all about. Without courts, there are just vigilante gangs out there, warring with one another for territorial control.

What is clear to me is that law enforcement personnel, even social workers, have become more and more sadistic over time. This tendency of human nature was clearly identified in the '70s at the psychology department in the University of Stanford (31). They divided students into two groups—guards and prisoners. In a very short period of time, the guards exhibited ever-increasing sadistic behavior toward the prisoners, including humiliation and beatings. This appears to have happened to the nation's police officers. Under the protection of the code of silence, they have become more and more sadistic toward the general public and are now the biggest threat to public safety. You are ten times more likely to be killed by police than by any accident.

*Law enforcement is compassionate work.*

People usually want to be police officers in order to help others and the community. The strategy of law enforcement is best when it de-escalates a conflict rather than overwhelm it with force. Law enforcement shines when it shows compassion to victims rather than judgment and humiliation and plays no favorites with regard to race, color, sex, religion, social standing while holding the law above all other considerations. This is the job of law enforcement; anything less is extortionist vigilantism.

The justice system has strayed from its mandate to protect and serve the public, to being the strong arm of banks and corporations.

It is clear to me that the court system favors those with deep pockets. In a legal contest, the side with the most money wins. This is absolutely contrary to the idea of justice for all. Police protect the corporations and impose the will of the banks and corporations upon the general population often in defiance of natural law, the constitution, and public will. The police are used to separate people from their property on fraudulent pretext and to silence dissent among the populace. In short, the justice system serves the banks and corporations more favorably than the general public. This is not a system for justice; it is a system for tyranny.

*When criminality is institutionalized, there is no law.*

# CHAPTER 17

# Taxes

Taxes are another drain on the personal income and raise the cost of living. Taxes are supposed to be used by government to provide necessary public service, like fire departments, police departments, and infrastructure, like bridge and road maintenance. Instead, they are used to maintain the interest on the national debt (32).

In the USA, federal taxes are to be apportioned by state population. That means the states with the highest populations pay the highest taxes, and these taxes are divided equally among said populations. States can tax transactions, as in a sales tax. You're not being taxed on the products but on the activity of selling stuff. An income tax is not part of the American way or the constitution. Even still, what you call the income tax is not really a tax on your income. Your income is used to determine how much tax you should pay, not directly taxed. Of course, this income is presumed to be from some taxable activity. In fact, the only income that is taxable is the income of a government employee (if you have a birth certificate and Social Security number, they consider you a government employee) (33). If you actually read the IRS tax return book, it tells you so—not very clear, but it's there.

The idea of taxes is like that of a bank. The community puts money into a common pot, and that money is used for the good and support of all. It pays for equipment, facilities, training, and payment for good public service, like the fire department, department of public works, water and power, waste disposal, etc.

The problem with taxes is that it is very easy to raise taxes so that the common person on the street has no money to pay anyone else or buy anything else. Taxation can be a lethal parasite on civilization, leaving its citizens weak, starving, and homeless.

Everyone thinks the federal income tax pays for federal government services, like national defense, national highway maintenance, national park service, and all the grants and subsidies as well as national health care, like Medicare, Medicaid, and Social Security. But in 1987 before he was shot, President Ronald Regan assigned the Grace Commission to see exactly where all of the nation's income tax was being spent (32). They concluded at that time, with the national debt around $3 trillion, that 100 percent of the collected national income tax went to pay the interest on the national debt or straight to the central bank and one dollar to public services.

So were does all the government's money come from? The same place all of the government's money has come from since 1776—import tariffs. The rest is made up of different kinds of credit, like treasury bonds and birth certificate bonds; these support the credit limit of the United States, known as the national debt. The collateral on US national debt is all of the personal and private property of everyone in the United States. As I have mentioned before, the purpose of the debt is to glean ownership. So in 1987, 100 percent of the public interest money was funneled into private hands.

CHAPTER 18

# Revolutions

According to recent history, we see a pattern of financial booms and busts (2). Every forty years or so, since the end of the US Civil War, we see a major change in the money system. We drifted from a 100 percent gold reserve stable money system, where the cash note was a receipt for gold or silver money in a bank vault, to a 40percent reserve, where every fifty dollars of paper money was backed by twenty dollars' worth of gold in the vault. Today there is nothing to base the paper money on except more paper money.

This has played out over and over again for the last five thousand years. "Hyperinflation coincides with war. As the nation goes to war, the currency supply explodes" (34). In ancient Greece, they went from gold coins to copper coins. In other places, they just create tokens and call it money. I imagine the reasoning behind this is because the spoils of war are intended to launder the counterfeit currency, which is printed for convenience to finance the war. Take the Spanish-American War in 1898. The USA won and collected the Spanish Empire: Cuba, the Philippines, and Puerto Rico.

*Remember, it's all about ownership.*

Just as the nation's money supply explodes to enable the production of war machines, it can also enable the production of everything else. It just depends on where the money is applied. Everyone asks, "If they have enough money for war, how come there is no money for education or health care or social services?" Because war is profitable and public services are not. When the government is privatized by private club interests, it serves its own interests first before the serving the body politic.

This creates the need for secret funding sources for unflattering military activities. This funding comes from the global drug trade and other illegal enterprises (35). It is laundered or legitimized through mutual funds (ESF) and international banks. This illegal currency may fund every terrorist organization and drug cartel, along with all the necessary politicians, police, and judges (justice system private clubs) required to protect the enterprise.

Everything the government, military, and intelligence agencies secretly do is funded this way. That's why the war on drugs, war on terror, etc., never make a dent in the illegal activities they are supposed to thwart. In fact, the opposite is true; there are more drugs available and more terrorism after these "wars on . . ." are declared (35).

The banks know more about you than any intelligence agency could hope to collect on you. They know what kind of and how much toilet paper you buy, how much booze you buy, everything. It's obvious they have used this information to gain leverage over politicians and law enforcement and are basically immune from prosecution. That's how they get away with such outrageous and obvious frauds.

Take the bailouts, for example.

Most recently, the US government laundered the counterfeit debt currency created during the real estate bubble by passing the debt and responsibility on to the general public via the "bailouts" that resulted in an increase of the national debt. The banks were unable to justify the fraud and could not default on themselves. After much theatrics, the government borrowed more money from the central bank to cover the gaps left over from the banking fraud. The largest gaps were between the homeowners and the mortgage lenders. Rather than pay the bailout money to the homeowners and relieve the problem, they paid huge lump sums to the lenders; the banks pocketed most of it by paying themselves huge bonuses, and the crisis continued. People were still losing their homes just as quickly as they were able to purchase them.

These American mortgages were the foundation of international mortgage-backed security investments. Countries like Iceland and Greece failed when the flood of defaults caused the value of those securities to evaporate. Greece is still trying to repay their losses. Meanwhile, the culprit banks are still protected and still committing the same fraud.

> In order to maintain central bank stability, there needs to be a balance between outstanding debt and the ability to pay the debt. The non-profit bank that creates money as debt-free compensation for labor is a perfect solution and a good start for making a better world for the new age.

Most recently, in Ukraine they have graduated from fraud to out and out robbery (36). The same week the new government took control of Kiev, all of the Ukraine reserve gold, about forty tons or $1.5 billion was taken out of the country and deposited in the New York Federal Reserve Bank. I am willing to bet that all the "financial aid" Kiev receives from the US, IMF, and World Bank is actually a loan of their own money back to them. There was not one word of protest or criticism in the worldwide mainstream media outlets about the obvious theft and resultant extortion. With military action continuing and escalating and no money to pay their soldiers with, Ukraine had to borrow for their own safety, which amounts to extortion. Meanwhile, in 2015 the state of Texas announced construction of its own gold depository for a billion dollars of gold bullion. *In mafia circles, 30 percent of your heist goes to the vic, in this case, the federal reserve in New York.*

# Conclusion

A debt-based currency system creates a life of working to pay bills instead of pursuing your happiness for most people. This financial treadmill is the cause of most suffering, stress, divorce and unhappiness and is falsely interpreted as result of political, religious or societal ills in general. The debt-based currency supply is the true culprit. It concentrates the currency supply in the upper classes and leaves the masses in financial drought. The only cure the present domestic and global banking systems offer is more debt. *The world is being run by corrupt private clubs for their own self-interest.* Currency is created by debt. There is always more debt than currency, so it is physically impossible to repay the debt. The purpose if this is to transfer ownership of the collateral for the debt, all the property to the bank.

*Labor is the only thing giving currency its value.* The traditional banks, a private club called the federal reserve system, will attempt to claim ownership of all present and future labor with perpetual debt created today.

*The debt is a fraud.* Government, a private club, pledge their citizens' labor to the bank with bonds originating from birth certificates.

*The police*, a private club, are the enforcers of the transfer of ownership.

*The courts*, a private club, illegally validates the fraud and is in conflict of interest.

Debt is a claim of ownership essentially.

All the present financial systems are organized to keep the individual in perpetual debt and thus maintain ownership of their labor.

We must build a method of creating money debt-free to stabilize everything and guarantee life, liberty, and the pursuit of happiness.

Money is all make-believe.

The only thing creating anything of wealth is labor. Money must be created from labor to ensure freedom and prosperity for all, for all time.

Fresh money is just as necessary as fresh food and water.

Economic growth is dependent on a steady supply of fresh currency that is not available when it is limited by physical gold. For true freedom to exist, every individual must possess the ability to make money with their labor without hindrance.

*The federal government is a private club of politicians that are monopolists of law. The judicial system is also controlled by private clubs.*

They use the one thing that could hold them accountable, law enforcement and the courts, to silence critics and prosecute whistle-blowers. They have institutionalized fraud. It is not difficult to reason out the flawed logic and fallacious arguments banks and corporations use to validate the system and justify their crimes. All this proves is that the entire financial system is, in fact, a farce.

Globalization is happening right now!

You see, humble reader, the corruption within the banks and corporations have destroyed the ideal of freedom for the loving American people. These banks and corporations have turned into gangsters that have institutionalized fraud, perjury, counterfeiting, usury, extortion, and murder to satiate their psychotic selfish desires for more.

Under tyranny or freedom, in poverty or abundance, the 99 percent will be united either way. It's up to us right here right now to do something about it.

The power to create money must be given to the public. Why? Because we see the results of the privateer bankers that manipulate the system for their own benefit to the detriment of life itself. Labor is the collateral of all debt when it is actually the only source of credit and value. You can be free of time in servitude and labor for yourself and those you love on your own terms, or you can labor under the club and the boot of gangsters. We are currently at a crossroads in human history. We can begin making life-saving changes right now. The choice is yours. If it's not you to decide, then who will choose for you? Read the next section carefully, for the entire future of humanity can be profoundly improved by what you decide.

The best course of action is for everyone to unite within one benevolent alternative to the corrupt and predatory financial and judicial systems, a *nonprofit central bank*! It's because governments and the police no longer protect society's most vulnerable citizens and the establishment has become predatory to those people it was built to protect.

The best method to create debt-free money available to everyone is to use a standard base labor currency.

I say let's claim what is genuinely ours—our labor, the true source of money and wealth.

*Butchers' Union Co. v. Crescent City Co., 111 U.S. 746 (1884)* affirms labor as property—and the most sacred kind of property. "Among these unalienable rights, as proclaimed in the Declaration of Independence is the right of men to pursue their happiness, by which is meant, the right any lawful business or vocation, in any manner not inconsistent with the equal rights of others, which may increase their prosperity or develop their faculties, so as to give them their highest enjoyment . . . It has been well said that '*the property which every man has is his own labor, as it is the original foundation of all other property so it is the most sacred and inviolable*'" (emphasis mine).

*We can use our inalienable right to possess ownership of our labor and create debt-free money for the individual citizen.*

It is simpler to create a benevolent, compassionate, and free financial system alternative that supports life, liberty, and pursuit of happiness for all of the nonviolent free people of the world. The collective reward will be *universal abundance for all*.

We have an undying will to be free.

*Your labor can be the source of your wages through the nonprofit central bank.*

I say "we the people" must nullify the corrupt system by instituting and participating in a free and fair currency system to use instead of the corrupt debt slavery being forced upon us. Instead of using debt as the method to create currency, *the people must be able to create money with their individual labor—the only real source of wealth and property.*

Your labor can be defined as anything you want it to be. You will be free to follow your bliss and pursue your happiness. You will no longer need permission from an employer or a bank to work. Your labor is as good as gold. Technology makes it possible.

| **Fractional Reserve Banking System** | **Public Nonprofit Central Bank** |
|---|---|
| It owns your labor. | You own your labor. |
| Employer owns the fruit of your labor. | You own the fruit of your labor. |
| You need permission to work from an employer. | You work at will without permission. |
| It creates unemployment. | It creates general employment. |
| It uses your birth certificate as collateral for a loan. | Your time and effort are collateral for a loan. |
| It uses a bond as a promise to pay. | It uses a bond as a promise to work. |
| It creates more debt than currency. | It creates more currency than debt. |
| The bank borrows from the people. | The bank borrows from itself. |
| It creates economic debt slavery. | It creates economic freedom. |
| It promotes crime. | It removes the motivation for crime. |
| It creates wars for profit. | It creates peace for profit. |
| It breaks families apart. | It keeps families together. |
| It's unstable. | It's stable. |
| It's impossible to pay the national debt. | It's possible to pay all debts. |
| It's vulnerable to failure—default. | It's immune to failure. |
| There are limited profits. | It has unlimited profits. |
| Beneficial services are not profitable/fundable. | Beneficial services are fundable and profitable. |
| It promotes destruction for profit. | It promotes creation for profit. |
| It limits production and trade. | Production and trade are unlimited. |
| It's prone to shortages. | It's prone to abundance. |

| | |
|---|---|
| Underwriters and insurers are vulnerable to failure. | It can underwrite and insure without the possibility of failure. |
| Fund pensions are not funded. | Pensions are funded. |
| It pays low wages to foster profits. | It fills the gap of low wages and cost of living. |
| Small businesses are prone to failure. | Small businesses are supported. |
| Availability of higher education is at great expense and debt. | Higher education is funded and subsidized for all. |
| Theirs is a militarized police force. | There's a reserve police of citizenry. |
| Military service is profitable. | Military service is discouraged. |
| It fosters mass human migration and immigration. | It removes the necessity to seek financial stability elsewhere. |
| It creates and inhibits the stability and development of the Third World as cheap labor source. | It empowers stability and development of the Third World. |
| Infrastructure is in decline and not funded. | Infrastructure is funded and well maintained |
| There are food supply shortages. | Food supply is abundant. |
| It promotes monopolies. | It promotes competition. |
| It's exclusive to those who have excess money. | It's inclusive of anyone willing to be free. |
| It's controlled by private interest. | It's controlled by the account holders. |
| It unfairly concentrates extreme wealth in the hands of a few private interests. | It fairly distributes wealth and wealth potential evenly among the populace. |
| It's despotic. | It's democratic. |
| It promotes slavery. | There is freedom. |

# PART II

# Fixes

# Model for a New Economic System with a Nonprofit Central Bank (NPCB)

This is an excerpt from an article from the London times circa 1862:

> If the mischievous financial policy which has its origin in North America shall become indurate down to a fixture, then that government will be able to furnish its own money without cost. It will pay off debts and be without debt. It will have all the money necessary to carry out its commerce. It will become prosperous without president in the history of the world. The brains and wealth of all countries will go to North America. That country must be destroyed or it will destroy every monarchy on the globe.

The excerpt from the article quoted above reveals several key truths about the perpetual problems in the debt-as-money system. First, being without debt is the key to prosperity. Second, a cost-free or debt-free money supply is the key to paying off debts and thriving commerce. Next, prosperity and a thriving economy are attractive attributes of a free society. Furthermore, a healthy and free economic system is the biggest threat to despotic or dictatorial rule from not only monarchies but plutocracies and every other form of tyranny not only in North America but all over the globe. And last but not least, the perpetual debt and the resultant ever-present boom and bust cycles of what we now call economic bubbles, recessions, and depressions are most probably deliberate and inflicted on the masses as a means of control rather than unpredictable pitfalls inherent in the "free market."

It also alludes to the fact that debt and all the monetary policies have from the beginning been designed to keep the rich richer and the poor poorer.

A public nonprofit central bank would be an independent third-party payer that can monetize an individual's time and effort without debt (cost), which could realize global prosperity without president in history. With the ability to convert time and effort into debt-free money transferred to the individual, a stable economic foundation is created upon which investment, insurance, and manufacturing platforms can be guaranteed. This means perpetual prosperity and eternal profits for all.

# Labor: As Good As Gold

The present system builds debt exponentially. Property is the collateral for this perpetual debt. If all the properties and deposits are seized by the bank, there will still be outstanding debt. This debt will be used as the claim to ownership of everyone's future property, especially their labor.

The principal way to avoid this trap is to claim the ownership of your personal labor before any bank, government, or corporation can do so.

A system that will enable debt-free or cost-free money is required to counter the debt-forfeiture machine. It is true that labor, any type of labor, is the foundation of all wealth, even gold, and is ideal to use as the new basis for a debt-free money supply.

If loans are the mechanism of perpetual debt, then labor must become the mechanism for perpetual credit. Even the value of gold is still just an agreement, an idea that is subject to change. Labor is the ultimate store of value. That means that its value will not change very much over time, so its value is stored. The only difference between golden commodity money and currency is its store of value (see the graphic on chapter 1 banking). Currency loses its value over time because it has no foundation beyond the debt contract used to create it. As long as there are people, there will be labor. As long as there is work to be done, labor will retain great value.

There are a number of effective ways that labor can be reasonably converted into money by the individual and will remain debt-free. Chiefly among them is the bond.

*Bond* (noun) is defined as

3. something that binds a person or persons to a certain circumstance or line of behavior: *the bond of matrimony.*
4. something, as an agreement or friendship that unites individuals or peoples into a group; covenant: *the bond between nations.*
5. binding security; firm assurance: *My word is my bond.*
6. *a sealed instrument under which a person, corporation, or government guarantees to pay a stated sum of money on or before a specific day.*
7. *any written obligation under seal.* (Dictionary.com, emphasis mine)

As I have stated before, the government uses your birth certificate as proof that it can collect taxes and fees. This creates a financial bond security that is used as collateral to increase the nation's money supply.

They pawn your labor without permission and without your knowledge or consent and offer no recourse for you to get it back or share the profits. To me, this seems like a shady and untrustworthy practice that becomes the foundation of more shady and untrustworthy practices hidden from public scrutiny. Basically, the government is selling your labor out from under you because the debt is impossible to repay and essentially selling you into slavery.

Since a bond can be just an agreement to pay, I see no reason why an individual person cannot go to a NPCB and float a bond for themselves. This contract between you and the NPCB can be used to create an account exactly as it is today. In order to get paid, the bank will give you a program like a bank card merged with payroll software that will allow you to report the amount of time you spent working that day or that week in hours and will convert the time into hard money, debt-free deposits at a fixed rate. It's easy as pie.

## A CURE FOR SLAVERY

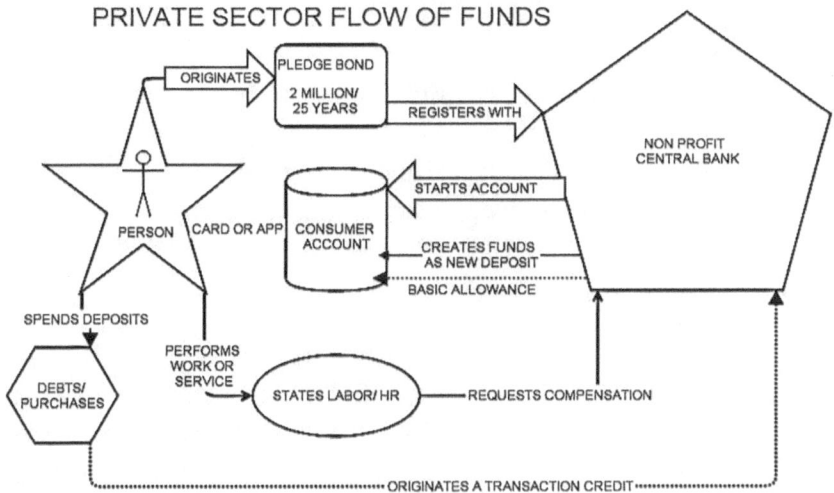

*Instead of going back to the gold standard and starting the entire corruption cycle over again, use the same principles of the gold standard with labor paramount to gold.*

In the gold standard, currency is based on gold's assigned value by weight. Thirty-five dollars an ounce was the measure that made the dollar the world's base currency after World War II (2). There were no foreign exchanges or fluctuating exchange rates at that time with stable gold prices. The stability of the fixed rate on the gold standard and the trust and confidence it inspired rebuilt the world after WWII and fostered growth and development until now.

A stable, free, and open standard is ideal for establishing freedom worldwide and replacing slavery with voluntary cooperative efforts.

*To those that say gold is better, I ask, "What comes first—the gold in the vault or the labor to dig it out of the ground?"*

In the first place, gold is limited, and the economy requires a constant supply of fresh, new money at a rate greater than gold can be sifted from the earth. Labor is limited only by the number of hours in the day and is available to everyone. Labor is the obvious choice for a free and fair basis for the money supply.

With all these wonderful electronic networks and the information superhighway, it is very simple to spend or create money anywhere at any time. Currency creation is available to anyone with a computer or cell phone. Electronic money can be the virtual gold in the mine, and every hour that a person spends working will be guaranteed money in the bank. In this new model, everyone everywhere can be instantly self-employed, insured, and earn credit to invest.

## There Is So Much Work to Do!

There is no shortage of work needed to be done just to heal and rebuild our suffering world. We are drowning in garbage. Garbage is now the apex predator in the oceans. It is responsible for the collapse of the oceanic food chain. Fundamentally, there is technology to recapture the oil in all the plastic trash, so it is a viable means to reclaim oil once the wells dry up (37).

In the present for-profit-only corporate-controlled society, it is simply not possible to properly handle all of the world's waste due to the vast amounts of labor involved in collecting and processing all the garbage and no way to profit from it presently. The endeavor is beneficial but not profitable. I bet there are millions of young people who would be willing to spend some time to clean up the global environment, but they are forced by financial necessity to work or seek out work under corporate dominion instead. Using labor instead of gold, *any* work is paid work.

If people can claim ownership of their labor and pay themselves debt-free, then the unemployment issue disappears. Suddenly, there is a vast abundance of labor that is neither devalued by profit-oriented, low-pay, low-staff requirements, high-intensity, and long-hour employment nor denied permission to work by an employer. (Can't get a job!) This abundance of labor would not be paralyzed by needing someone else to pay for one's time and effort. Everyone would be fundamentally self-employed.

# Earnings: Creating Money from Labor

Myself, and many others in the world, have been raised with a strong work ethic. We all know we have to work for what we want. There are no free rides. The problem with unemployment and homelessness is not the idea that "those people" are lazy or don't want to work. The problem is, we all need permission to work, necessitated by the fact we need somebody to work for. If everyone owns his or her labor and can create/make money with their work, then everyone everywhere is automatically self-employed by default. Some may cheat and claim pay for work they did not do, but that is their karma and will not affect anyone else. Most people around the world are honest and hardworking people. If they are given a chance to earn fair pay for good work, I am sure we will all be amazed at the wonderful things people would be happy to do and create.

*One way to claim ownership of your labor could be a standard pay scale worldwide.*

Take a look at the global prosperity that happened after WWII and apply the key factors: (a) gold was fixed at thirty-five dollars per ounce and applied across the world, and (b) global currencies were fixed to the gold standard (9). This honest and fair agreement created economic conditions that were clear and easily understood. It gave everyone in the world something to work with.

What if by similar agreement, generic labor is valued at forty dollars an hour? We will have the same key factors:

1. There will be a good fixed rate evenly applied across the world.

2. Since labor is the principal source of all wealth, all the currencies could easily be stabilized by the labor standard.
3. This honest and fair agreement could create economic conditions that are clear and easily understood. Labor is a better standard than gold because it is unlimited. As long as there are people, their labor will be a source of value.

Let's look at a forty-dollars-per-hour labor standard. So you, the concerned and otherwise unoccupied and free person, take it upon yourself to go out and pick up some trash cluttering up a creek or whatever for four hours one morning. All you have to do is log on to the system app, program, or webpage, just like online banking, and fill out your pay voucher like any temp agency uses and hit Send. Wait for it, and the next text you receive from your bank states you just received $160—debt-free, tax-free dollars. Then you go to work at a job where you log another $40 per hour in addition to regular (probably minimum) wages paid to you by the employer.

Perhaps you enjoy making a table in your workshop. Log the time and get paid instantly.

The new system will resemble the present system with a few key changes:

1. Labor will create money debt-free.
2. The individual will be able to contract a personal bond security with the bank. Instead of the bank creating debt and giving some currency to the individual, the individual creates/earns/makes the money with his or her labor (time and effort), and the bank issues a deposit at the standard rate in return.

It's a win-win situation because the individual owns his or her labor and will be immediately compensated. The bank will receive a bond security that it can trade in the stock market, loan, or sell as it has always done and will create and receive hard-money deposits that it can use for valuation and perpetual loan reserves. This labor foundation can underwrite all other investments and insurance companies and banks worldwide.

As long as there are people, the bank will have a source of real money, created from the source of all wealth—*labor*. The banking industry will not be vulnerable to failure, even from large-scale fraud. If the bank overextends by loaning out more than it has, all it has to do is wait a day and let the reserves fill up.

This idea only hits a snag when you have to consider that the for-profit banks are never going to give up their claim of ownership on your labor very easily. A new public bank may be necessary if the present banks resist popular change.

One clear solution is a *nonprofit central bank* (NPCB) that creates money debt-free for the individual. No debt would mean the elimination of all external financial claims of ownership by the government and the bank. An NPCB can be a service platform for creation of money debt-free for anyone anywhere. Like rainfall in the forest or a well in the town square, a nonprofit central bank can be free to use for the debt-free compensation of labor.

## Earnings Bond

A good way to standardize labor creating money is through an individual bond or pledge. This can be accomplished using the same logic and contracts already in use between the US treasury and the Fed. Using the public NPCB system, an individual can either legally reassign their birth certificate bond from the federal reserve to the NPCB or, more simply, create a new individual bond with the NPCB, using their birth certificate, driver's license, professional license or certificate, or honest pledge in the amount they plan to create with their work.

These bonds would be used by the *nonprofit central bank* as a financial basis to create currency for individual compensation on demand without cost. Similar to the present system where bonds are collateralized for debt-based currency by the government through the FED, these new bonds can be collateralized for money on demand by the individual through the NPCB.

The individual can pledge to work for a number of years for a standard hourly rate, which will create debt-free money from their labor along the way. As the individual works on a daily basis, the funds are created as debt-free deposits in their account.

As the for-profit fractional reserve bank can create currency from loans up to 90 percent of deposits, so would the *nonprofit central bank* be able to create currency up to 90 percent of personal bonds (as securities) and deposits to fund basic consumer income and public sector services for example. This is the bank borrowing from the people without risk.

This creates a positive feedback loop that perpetuates the money supply debt-free. The currency created debt-free can be used to enable public sector enterprise, such as nonadverse environmental protections, toxic-waste disposal, recycling, green energy, sustainable living, and organic farming. Anything that is necessary and beneficial but presently not profitable could become fundable and profitable.

It can work like this: A person files a $1.6 million personal bond with the bank to open an NPCB labor account. This is a projection of how much work that person can do at $40 per hour, forty hours a week, forty weeks a year for twenty-five years, for example. So the person now has potentially $1.6 million to collect one hour at a time, debt-free. The bank has a twenty-five-year $1.6 million bond per individual that it can create another $1.35 million from whenever it needs to.

The individual can perform self-styled work or work for someone else or both. In order to uphold a reasonable work ethic, the bond contract with the public NPCB could be in a probationary period until the individual fulfills 10 percent of the bond amount if self-styled labor or 5 percent if employed. For example, forty dollars per hour for eight hours a day, five days a week for one hundred weeks for self-styled or fifty weeks if employed. Upon fulfillment, the account will be considered vested; 80 percent of the remaining bond amount could then be available to the individual and the NPCB as credit and open for investments and loans respectively. In this way, people actually earn their credit through diligent work rather than service the perpetual debt charade known as a FICO score.

Labor into money could create hard-money deposits as good as gold. The personal bonds could be a security for currency creation the same way as cash was originally created from gold deposits. The labor deposits could be the foundation of the money supply, and the bonds could be stretched and worked in order to accomplish expansion of public goods and services in furtherance of life, liberty, and pursuit of happiness for all, debt-free! As long as there are people following their bliss, there would be a stable supply of fresh debt-free money for the system to work with.

*Everyone can make money, literally.*

In short, the individual would be able to perform their labor of choice and receive payment in debt-free money, just like the act of digging gold out of the ground. The public *nonprofit central bank* can support debt-free money created on demand, without limit as to the type or character of the work performed, and will ignore other sources of personal compensations (pay) a person may receive. *You can double-dip!* Simply put, get paid from your employer and from your NPCB account.

If you already have a job but feel your time is worth more than you are getting paid from your employer, the NCPB can make up the difference debt-free. Individuals can decide what is best for them in their own situation. They would be self-regulated by their personal ethical and spiritual morality. In this way, Dr. Martin Luther King's dream of people being judged foremost by the content of their character could be a worldwide reality. If some individuals wish to cheat and get something for nothing, they would not cause a shortage or loss for others.

## Service Is Labor

"If my computer is working, I am working" (Julian Colberg).

In today's world, the user is charged a fee for use of a system or thing. These are described as convenience fees (or service fees), website registration fees, and even ATM fees. These fees are used to pay for the manufacture and upkeep of the system or thing being used, as well as provide profit for the creator of said system or thing.

In the NPC system, the use of a service or thing can pay a credit to the manufacturer, owner, and in some cases, the user. Like a royalty payment or activity tax, the activity of use can be considered labor in some situations. For example, use of a public or government building, roadway, bridge, park, or bank can generate a credit for the thing being used. Instead of or in addition to paying for parking at the park, the funds collected go to the upkeep of the park, the users of the park are recorded, and the volume of use generates a payment for the owners, builders, workers, and investors of the park.

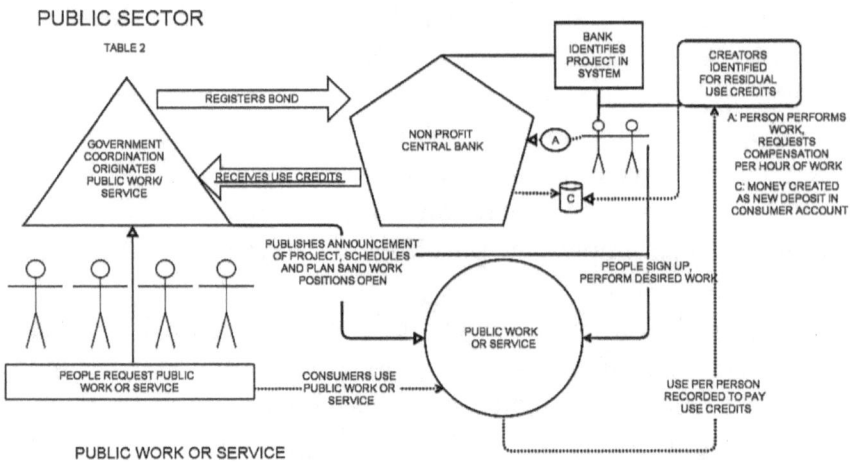

In the example graphic above, first, the people request a public work or service. The NPCB, in coordination with the local governments, generates a bond for the public work or service. The NPCB then publishes the project to attract participants in the form of workers, designers, and investors. These participants register and perform their labor to fulfill the bond. People use the public work or service and thus a use credit is paid to the registered creators similar to royalty.

This means the bank can pay itself for the service of facilitating commerce. The code for the banking program can create a usage credit for itself. It would be similar to a virus that skims the fractions of a penny off every transaction. Instead it creates a few pennies' credit with every transaction/use. These pennies can all be created (paid) in a consumer bank mutual fund that is allowed to borrow from itself to cover the daily reserve balances. If there is a shortfall, the bank can credit itself from the labor bond securities.

Similar to "get cash back with every purchase" credit card promotions, the bank could pay itself as well as the consumer and the supplier for that matter. This increases the volume of bank currency from which more credits could be generated. For example, the bank can create a transaction credit for every transaction completed through the system, the idea being that the labor of using the system and the labor of the system service itself can also create money. The more transactions, the more money the bank creates for itself. (I mean, really, since the Fed uses its fractional reserve bullshit parade to create slavery, starvation, poverty, and crime, it seems logical to invent some proactive protocols that can employ and empower everyone, using a similar rationale. It's all make-believe after all.)

This same principal can be applied to all service industries:

1. *Health care.* A hospital can create money for itself by treating people. The more people it services, the more money it earns for itself.
2. *Education.* The more students completing courses, the more money it earns for itself. The concept is that the more a service is utilized, the more it earns. More usage means more earnings.

Another good example is highway maintenance. Right now, the money for roadway construction and maintenance comes from taxes collected from vehicle fees or taxes or gasoline taxes passed on to the consumer with higher gas prices and bond measures in general. In the new system though, workers could earn what they want by doing the work of building or repairing the roadway through the NPCB. The city, state, and/or federal government can pay itself through the NPCB every time the road is used by anything or anyone. It would work like a reverse toll road. It can even include residual payments to the workers who build the road, like a movie star getting paid every time his or her movie is shown on TV. The travelers are counted and a debt-free sum is generated and deposited in the appropriate accounts. In this way, infrastructure perpetually generates the funds necessary for maintenance and upgrades.

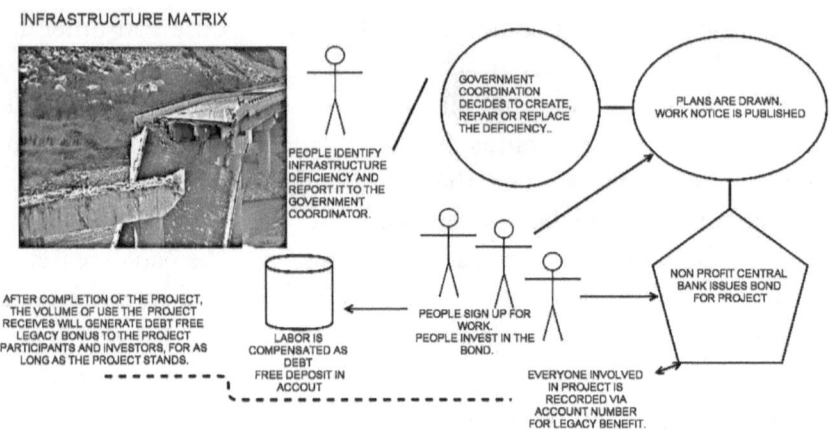

INFRASTRUCTURE MATRIX

## The New Consumer Class

Because the economy is so important to everyone from the lowest of the low to the ultrarich, the ability for everyone to consume products and services unhindered should be upheld as an unalienable right.

Economic security is national security. Economic security depends on a stable money supply and the rate of consumption. When goods and services are consumed liberally, the economy is booming. When people do not have enough money to consume liberally, the economy is in recession. In order to ensure that there is liberal consumption for the economy, several countries have started to give their citizens a "basic income" for the sole purpose of supporting consumption.

This basic income idea could foster a new financial class, a consumer class of citizen. This can be funded by transaction credits, like reverse consumption taxes, paid by the bank to itself as described in service as labor, for example.

Your first job is to obey the laws and not hurt anyone and, secondly, to buy stuff. This new economic social class could eliminate the lower class and unite the upper and middle classes in the consumer class.

The *nonprofit central bank* (NPCB) can provide debt-free money as a basic living allowance (or basic income) from its own transaction earnings. Ideally, this should be available to anyone who has a criminal history free of violent crime for the past two years. I think this qualification is good for high-crime areas because it reinforces lawful behavior. Crime will not pay.

Coincidentally, the consumer can create more money with the labor of consumption. In other words, you can pay yourself when you shop. Anything is possible.

Whether you're a billionaire philanthropist or heavy-machine operator, you're a consumer first. Debt-free money flooding the grass roots of every society everywhere is fertile soil for eternal profits. Everyone will be able to consume goods and services as long as they draw breath.

*Debt-free funds provided by the nonprofit central bank could be used to pay off debts.* What we need to learn about this repeating cycle of hyperinflation is that *hyperinflation is necessary* and required, but at the same time, it is also doomed because the debt hyperinflates above the currency supply. This is what some might call a negative feedback loop: where the process gets weaker and weaker with every cycle until it fails.

*Labor can create a positive feedback loop where the process gets stronger and stronger with every cycle.* To change from a debt-centric to credit-centric system, a positive feedback loop is necessary for sustainability. These labor-created funds or earnings will eventually bridge the gap and pay off the debt as well as create a surplus to stabilize the economy. The money earned will not lose its value because labor will not lose its value. Currency will lose its importance and overwhelming influence in our lives and clear the way for the pursuit of true happiness.

# Unlimited Potential

We have the technology to completely remove pollution and waste from the globe; so far it has just not been profitable to do so. A *non-profit central bank* (NPCB) with its labor-creating wealth can make everything profitable forever. The labor creates the money just as the labor of digging gold out of the ground creates money, and it's much easier. Every shovel pitched is pay dirt. Every hour spent productively, every picture painted, every sweater knitted, every piece of litter collected can pay nicely.

No longer would banks have the ability to fail. Another day's work means another day's pay no matter what. More pay means more deposits. There would not be a need for a run on the bank. The bank could not lose your money because you create it as you work.

Your labor bond is a promise to do something. It can be anything because whatever you do will create money. If the banks accounting goes awry, no one loses anything, and it is an internal accounting error and solved by internal accounting adjustments.

In this next section, I really push the ideal envelope. It is not written in stone, so these are just some basic ideal concepts, and one should not throw the baby out with the bathwater.

# Design

In order to make sure that the *nonprofit central bank service* cannot be manipulated to enslave any future generations, it should be divided into sectors. One sector could be designated as a private sector. That would be the realm of private personal finances and transactions that would remain immune to government manipulation or interference. Any necessary changes would be permitted only after a fourth-fifths majority vote of all account holders.

The government could have its own designated sector, along with business and industry, a designated public sector. This would be similar to the three divisions or branches of the US government: the executive branch, which are the president and his or her cabinet; the legislative branch, which is the senate and House of Representatives, also known as Congress; and the judicial branch, which is the members of the Supreme Court.

## The Private Sector

With the new NPCB in place, the private sector would create a compartment for each private person. This sector would create money from an individual's labor for the individual who labored. It could also be the source of funds for a basic consumption allowance (basic income) and education/public service bonus credits (table 3). I would suggest a requirement of a criminal history free of violent crime for two years. This would make lawful behavior payable and could inspire crime-ridden geographical regions to follow a rule of law.

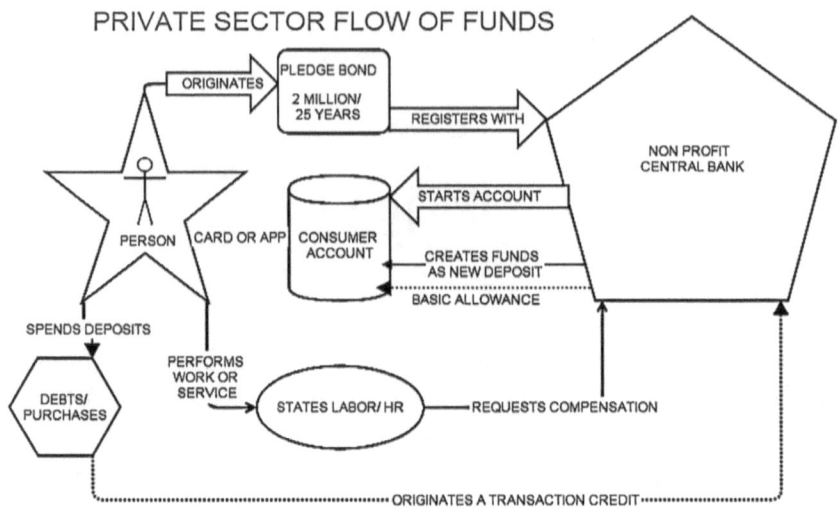

In the NPCB system, the basic income disbursements would come straight from the NPCB as monthly deposits into the individual's consumer account (table 1). This account could function like a standard checking account—without fees, of course. With every transaction, the NPCB will originate a transaction credit to the consumer, the merchant, and the NPCB itself.

The consumer's transaction credit can be deposited back into the consumer account or held in reserve as a prepaid line of credit. Alternately, the consumer transaction credit can be used as a payment to an existing loan or credit account.

The merchant transaction credit would be directly deposited into the merchant's credit account and used as a deposit reserve for business subsidy. The business subsidy would be paid out to merchants on a quarterly basis to guarantee at least 20 percent in profits. In order to qualify for this benefit, a merchant must lower all prices by 10 percent. The NPCB will use the merchant transaction credit reserve to subsidize quarterly gross receipts up to 20 percent profit, using the 10 percent reserve / 90 percent credit rule. Annual profits in excess of 500 percent will revert back to the NPCB.

The NPCB credit to itself would originate a transaction credit into a central fund as a reserve deposit. These transaction credits will be the basis for the basic income payments to qualifying individuals and would be generated using the 10 percent reserve, 90 percent credit standard used by the fractional reserve banking system today. The NPCB will borrow from itself and pay itself as it is used.

There comes a gray area with regard privacy and the basic income and the education / public service bonus credits (table 3). These invite government intrusion because the basic income eligibility requires a criminal history check and the education / public service bonus credits will require institutional cooperation from the justice system, the Department of Education, and health care systems already in place. Additionally, governmental oversight should be preserved for eligibility requirements and licensure in order to maintain high-quality standards of care and competence of service. Debt-free money should not replace quality-dedicated service with token standards and halfhearted effort.

*Private sector funds are not controlled by governments or corporations.*

With a NPCB labor account, the private person can access and spend these funds as they see fit without threat of seizure or forfeit for any reason. They are created by the work of the person, whatever that person sees fit to call work. It is an individual's private business, all of which the bank and the economy can use.

The privacy and possession of the labor account is absolute. The hard money created with an individual's labor is as good as gold in NPCB system. There must never be any requirement to open a labor account other than the individual's willingness to work as evident by the sealed bond accepted by the NPCB. There must never be a limit to the type or duration of work performed. No one will be able to tell you what you can or cannot do to earn your money in a NPCB labor account. Furthermore, the labor account will be structured like a revocable living trust. Access to the account, any limitations and beneficiaries are specified by the original account holder, who seals the bond with the NPCB.

When the NPCB labor account holder has earned 10 percent of the bond's face value, the bond will be considered vested and insured by NPCB. A vested labor account will have a line of credit available similar to an equity line of credit to the face value of the bond.

If for some reason the unvested NPCB labor account holder dies and has no heirs, the hard-money funds will revert to NPCB as a reserve for bond insurance credits within the NPCB.

If a vested NPCB labor account holder dies,

1. with heirs, the funds are distributed as specified by the account trust;
2. without heirs, the hard-money funds revert to the state NPCB accounts as credit reserves.

The NPCB will use the labor bond for security and valuation purposes.

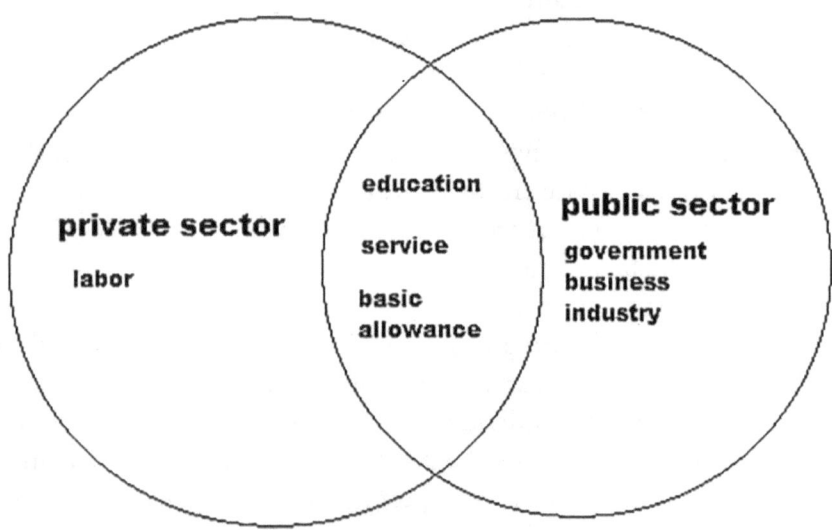

## The NPCB Public Sector

The public sector will have full public transparency and accountability. There is a designated business/industrial sector. Its funding creates compartments for business startup, stabilization, modernization, and environmental upgrades to reduce or eliminate toxic waste (table 2).

The basis of these funds can be hard-money deposits created from labor that has reverted to the NPCB, professional license bonds, and business project and construction bonds in addition to private sector investors. This money can be for business credits for building construction, infrastructure integration, and everything business and industry need to get up and going.

Business/industrial *startup* funds can be provided debt-free to competent entrepreneurs and inventors in order to further serve and expand existing markets to break up monopolies and expand development. Of course, relevant competency as demonstrated by appropriate education degrees and licensing as required by the Government Coordination Office would be prudent.

Business/industrial *stabilization* funds can be provided to business/industry to curtail retail price inflation and guarantee both profits and operation costs. If the banks can bail themselves out without blowback, then that option should be available to every business.

Business/industrial *modernization* funds can be provided to existing businesses/industries to upgrade their environments and retrofit for a lower energy consumption, lower toxic-waist production, and lower carbon footprint. This can include upgrading facilities to solar and wind power and whatever future technology has to offer.

With a NPCB, a business/industrial sector of *environmental upgrade* funds can start, sustain, and expand a pioneering environmental industry focused entirely on production, deployment, and utilization of environmental processes and products. Cleaning up the environment can be a vastly profitable sector with a nonprofit central bank. All of the industrial waste currently being generated is now the raw material for this pioneering sector. All the litter and trash become new resource commodities. Funds can be used to research new techniques of practical processing and reclaiming what can be used and creation of environmentally conscious methods of storage and disposal for the rest.

I recently heard about a lake that would require $6 million to clean up and restore all its shores to fresh potable water standards.

A nonprofit central bank could fund this, pay everyone involved in the project, and pay for the maintenance thereafter. With the lake restored and well maintained, the NPCB use credit could pay residuals to everyone involved every time someone enjoys the clean lake.

## The NPCB Public Sector: Manufacturing

NPCB funds applied to clean manufacturing and product longevity can drastically alter the manufacturing landscape. These funds can be used to retrofit existing facilities as well as create new manufacturing facilities in underserved areas. The retrofit can modernize the facilities for lower energy consumption and lower waste production.

The NPCB can also pay a residual bonus to the manufacturer, executives, and workers for every year a given unit is in operation. For example, you have a clean, green factory that produces a durable good like a refrigerator, and you sell a refrigerator to a retailer. When that retailer sells that unit to the end user, the details are submitted, and for every year the unit is in operation, the manufacturer will get a bonus. These annual bonuses can be used however the company sees fit.

*So gone will be the days of designed for the dump and start of the days of designed for the ages.* The longer the product lasts, the more money it will make for the manufacturer. Fewer natural resources will be consumed, and the consumer will have wider variety of products available. With a bonus structure like this, it is possible to simply give the units to consumers and collect the annual bonuses indefinitely. The earning potential for durable goods becomes dependent on the durability and longevity of the good. Unlimited longevity of use means unlimited profits.

Manufacturing funded by the NPCB will create a financial foundation for higher employee wages and benefits—especially pensions and, of course, eternal profits (table 7).

## The NPCB Public Sector: Labor

Because of technological advancements, the need for labor is decreasing, and the population is increasing. There are simply fewer and fewer jobs to go around. So instead of rising the retirement ages and forcing the few who have jobs to work longer over their lives, this system allows for fewer years working with long-term income applied from the fruits of their labor. This means a worker may only have to make things for five or ten years before the income produced by the use of their product is satisfactory. Then they can give up their seat to someone else who will only have to work for a few years. This gives everyone a chance to earn a long-term residual income.

A bonus can also be paid to the actual worker whose own hands and skill went into the manufacturing of anything in the system. Assembly line workers and trades people making anything will be able to receive bonuses for the continued end-user use of the item they created. This will motivate high quality of workmanship in everything manufactured as well as create a retirement income basis for the individual workers.

Labor in service to the trades and arts can pay the craftsperson for the labor of the job and a royalty for the length of time the work remains operational. The artist can perform on the street and get paid for his or her time based on expertise in addition to what is collected in the hat. If an artist is commissioned to paint a mural, they can receive not only the hourly labor from the NPCB but a bonus for the creation of the work (the commission) and also a royalty for how long the work lasts (table 8).

The main idea of the labor sector is, if you built it, *it is yours*.

# The NPCB Public Sector: Education / Public Service Bonus

Education sector funds can provide all levels of education to everyone debt-free. Funding for this sector pays for upgrades to existing facilities as well as for the creation of new eco-friendly facilities, supplies, teacher and student bonuses, research and development of new technology—all of which can be provided debt-free.

For example, a community wants another school to reduce class sizes. They request debt-free funding from the NPCB by creating a construction credit bond for the structure—to be repaid by the use of the new school. The Government Coordination Office posts the project on its board and opens the project to private investors as well. The construction bond funds and investors purchase the building materials. Labor gets paid from the NPCB labor account and salary from the project. Everyone involved in the process is recorded, and as long as the new school is in use, they will receive a residual payment.

The students will come with bond-based funds like the labor account but with their educational goals as the bond amount. For example, a doctorate bond in the ball park of US$300,000 per doctorate student. This bond will monetize the education credits a student will earn by anticipating the income they will generate from their labor once they put their education to use (just like the government using your birth certificate to monetize the anticipated taxes and fees they will collect from you over your life).

The student will earn a money credit from the NPCB for attending classes and a permanent residual bonus for every unit completed to vest and then complete the bond. The education service provider (school's account) will use this bond once vested to create 90 percent more debt-free currency (credit) for use if necessary.

This way, the labor of going to school will pay the student for both attendance and for the units completed. The number of students going through the school will pay the school construction project residuals. Just as the use of durable goods will pay the manufacturer in the example above, so will the completed units of education pay the student over their lifetime. In addition, the instructors can receive bonuses for every student that graduates besides their labor and salary from the school.

Beneficially, if a student studies subjects of societal benefit—such as emergency medicine, firefighting, and administration of justice—and promises to use his or her knowledge on a "should the need arise" basis or per diem, then the student can additionally receive a monthly service provider consideration. For those students who perform above and beyond the call of duty when the need arises, their instructors can also be rewarded with bonuses or laurels (table 9).

*This will reinforce the importance of education as well as honor the teachers, remove the debt burden associated with education, and expand access to education for everyone.*

## The NPCB Public Sector: Health Care

The NPCB health care sector funds can finance all aspects of health care for everyone, fund upgrades of existing facilities, fund the creation of new facilities in underserved rural areas, and fund research and development of new treatment techniques and disease prevention (table 9).

Providers can create a professional practice bond for the amount they would expect to make from the practice if needed. The central bank can then create 90 percent of that amount for immediate use. The facility overhead can be paid by how many patients they see and how many of those remain healthy.

Similar to HMO funding, a clinic funded by the NPCB health care sector will receive a monthly stipend for every patient enrolled. Additionally, the clinic can receive debt-free subsidies for every patient treated, every procedure performed, all lab tests, etc. The labor of practicing medicine will generate the staff salaries paid by the NPCB. The cost of treatment could be shared or be cost-free to the clinic.

Maternity leave, stress leave, occupational and physical therapies would all be subsidized and offered with little or no cost to the patients by the NPCB. These situations would be covered easily by the basic income and consumption earnings.

Suddenly, all the beneficial things that are not profitable under a debt-as-money system become profitable and sustainable when a labor-as-money system is implemented.

## The Government Sector and the NPCB

The function of government would naturally transition from favoring private clubs to administration of public endeavors. The NPCB Government Coordination Office can work in tandem with existing city planners to mediate real estate development. In this,

I mean that through use of existing permit requirements, zoning, building codes, and environmental impact studies, the Government Coordination Office of the NPCB would focus on providing necessary services to all and prohibit over development.

With the sudden availability of unlimited funding for public works and private business, a coordinating government would see to it that there is not a stadium constructed every half mile and make sure that there are enough hospitals, schools, and markets to satisfy demand via population densities adequately.

Coordination of resources and labor in the public sector would be achieved by a Government Coordination Office website, where individuals and organizations could post projects and activities that need materials and staffing.

Quality of service could be enforced by official GCO publications and guidelines for producers and service providers to maintain consistently high standards.

Government sector funds from the *nonprofit central bank* can fully fund high-quality maintenance of infrastructure and public service, like emergency medical services, fire services, and social services.

All the things they used to collect taxes for would now have unlimited funding and the need for taxation becomes obsolete. The labor of administration would create salaries, and volume can create residual pay for the administrators.

For example, imagine you are an administrator for a city planner and you authorize a development of a new park. The landscaper gets paid for his or her work in the design, the workers get paid for their labor, and everyone involved can get a little extra for every person who enjoys the park as long as the park exists. The more public projects built and used, the more everyone gets paid.

These are just a few of many possible sectors and subsectors of the *nonprofit central bank*. I intentionally leave out military for reasons I will explain later on in this book.

# Revelations

With a labor-as-money system, job creation could never be easier because everyone participating is instantly self-employed. Want to clean up your local park? Go out. Do what you do for as long as you want. Log into the website or use your gadget app and get paid. Want to develop new technology to process industrial waste into something useful or just not harmful? Do the work and get paid. Selling it later is extra.

If there is a will, there is now a way with virtually unlimited funding by NPCB. Just write it up and do it; the funding is there for you. Did you see a documentary about trash on a distant island that is killing everything there and feel like doing something about it? Organize a trip, gather support, pay yourselves whatever you need to make it worth your while, and do it; the funding is there for you. Need a new hospital in your area? The funding is there. Need a new university? The funding is there. Need a new bridge or highway? The funding is there. It's the desire to do the work and the actual work that creates the money, debt-free.

## Imagining the Possibilities

A *nonprofit central bank* can reinvent commerce, so it is not a game with winners and losers but a process of exchange. In the future, they do not expect you to pay at the cashier when you buy groceries. You will just walk in, fill your cart with products, and walk out (38). The moment you cross the doorway on your way out, technology will itemize your basket, identify you, and debit your account accordingly. You might not even be aware of how much something costs when you buy it.

With a labor-as-money system, this same thing can work to keep prices low. In addition to you paying the store for the goods you want, the store can receive a subsidy for the labor of the service it provides as measured by the number of items it moves. So as you leave a store, the store receives a credit to its account from the central bank. You may just have to pay a token membership fee annually, if anything at all.

With all the larceny and fraud currently indigenous in both in government and banking, why not just accept the fact that the debt banking system does not work and make a reasonable system that has no losers? Since no one is being punished for anything, let's keep it that way.

With a *nonprofit central bank*, there is no debt or need for the bank to own anything, and the government will not need to collect taxes. Your private transactions would be your private transactions. No one would have to know who you are dealing with or why. Privacy would become institutionalized.

A *nonprofit central bank* supporting a labor-as-good-as-gold process can make any endeavor profitable.

An alternative to the detailed *nonprofit central bank* outlined above, the NPCB can adopt a supporting role by compensating wages and labor costs to employers. Imagine a factory where the owners reap all the profits they want and the workers receive wages and benefits they feel are desirable. The factory can claim a compensation for labor and benefits costs from the NPCB in order to offset profit losses, and/or the individual worker can claim fair compensation adjustment from the *nonprofit central bank*.

Did your mine get shut down because of political reasons? No reason to starve and riot—just claim wage compensation insurance for labor and stay home and play with the kids. It's very simple, fair, and humane. The *nonprofit central bank* can fund it. Consider it automatic unemployment / disability insurance that you don't have to pay into. It is automatically activated by your participation.

Clearly, the possibilities are endless. We can create a better world for the new age. It will take some work, but it will work. There is a colossal amount of work our planet needs to heal and recover. We have enough people to do it, and together we can do it all without undo hardship.

With a *nonprofit central bank*, the labor, any labor, will create money debt-free for the individual anywhere.

We can see an end to poverty and suffering everywhere in the world.

Empower the individuals to work for pay, and they will do amazing things for themselves and the planet. They can build a house for themselves and pay themselves to do it. They can grow their own crops and pay themselves to do it, and they can do anything they want without being limited by needing employment.

*Remember, money is completely make-believe* (2).

I hear of economists speaking of the impossibility of perpetual growth on a finite planet. I disagree because the key resource in question—money—is completely imaginary and therefore unlimited. The economic problems of designing for the dump would be eliminated by longevity compensations to manufacturers. As mentioned above, the producer could receive a reward for every unit produced that is still in use annually. In this way, a company can have perpetual economic growth without constantly consuming real resources.

## Other Benefits

A *nonprofit central bank* can fund environmental protection debt-free. Amazon deforestation is of global concern. They can be paid not to destroy the lungs of the earth. As with all environmental destruction, the companies involved can be paid to stay home. The demand for the raw materials can be met by other more readily sustainable materials.

A *nonprofit central bank* can eliminate all taxes. In the theocracies, they collected taxes to pay for huge public works, like temples, aqueducts, and pyramids. States, cities, and towns will be able to just name their price and leave the people's money alone.

## Alternative Limits

I acknowledge that a lot of these concepts are idealistic, but they are very real and possible if people can get past their cognitive dissonance—perhaps some gradual stepping away from the present idea that shortage is necessary in order to get anything done. The shortage is necessary for the private clubs to maintain control.

Some limits here and there, negotiated and argued by politicians, and bar stool economists will probably continue for some years to come before the general society realizes that it is just a game we create for ourselves and there does not have to be any losers.

Some examples of arbitrary alternative limits are the following:

1. *The Fibonacci alternative.* The funds available for consumption activities can expand quarterly, using the Fibonacci sequence. If enough funds are not spent in the previous quarter, expansion does not occur.
2. *The 500 percent solution.* All participating businesses would waive profits over 500 percent back to the bank. This in turn can be used as a basis to create more currency.
3. *Hard work = hard cash.* Create a flexible schedule of wages for self-supervised self-employment and for skilled versus unskilled labor. This should satisfy those that require reassurance that they are not working harder than their neighbor or harder than they have to and that everyone else is not just sitting on their hands, collecting money. Soon, the young ones will realize that the harder they work or the more stuff they do, the more wealth they gain, and the world will get better as a result.
4. *Thou shalt not hoard.* Irrational hoarding of resources should be discouraged and limited by government coordination.
5. *If it ain't broke, don't fix it.* Government-administered permits and code enforcement for all new construction as well as sustainable energy plans for new developments should continue.

6. *Whoa! Nelly.* Local and state coordination is necessary for large projects so there isn't a stadium every two miles.
7. *Baby wants it! Baby gets it!* Funds available to children are scheduled with the Fibonacci sequence. If the spending limits are not met the previous period, expansion does not occur.

# Projected Impact Review

I touched on these obvious benefits of the NPCB labor-to-money system in the introduction. I want to elaborate further on some important subjects. These subjects plague society and derive from the financial shortages created by the current debt-as-money fractional reserve system.

Here are the positive impact predictions from the NPCB on different areas/sectors.

## Crime

The source of almost all crime is the perceived shortage of money. The surface tension of debt across society in general with everyone beholden to the bank forces people to seek out currency from their neighbors in order to pay their debt interest. If money is readily available to all natural law-abiding citizens, then violent crime will not be an option, even in the most desperate circumstances, and monetary crime can be nullified.

Lawful behavior of citizens in cooperation with one another will be more profitable than criminal enterprise in this system. Every person will have the ability to work and get paid on a daily basis. You would handle your own private account, and you would be the only one to see it. You could pay yourself for your work when you choose.

This will remove much conflict in society. The individual will become the principal, self-reliant source of money. The need to panhandle and steal from one another will disappear, because everyone will be empowered with self-employment and will be able to pay themselves. If someone wants to exaggerate their numbers, then that is their karma. It doesn't have to be mine or anybody else's concern. Most crimes of money will cease to exist. Only crimes of passion and mental illness would persist.

## Families

I myself am pro-choice when it comes to a mother's decision to carry a child or not. She has to physically do it; it's up to her.

However, in my life, whenever I have been confronted with such decisions, my financial abilities were of foremost concern—not my happiness, not my love or the expression of that love embodied in the fetus. Moreover, could I pay for it? If everyone owned their labor, how many would have had the baby?

Could I be happy struggling and stressing to make inadequate or just getting-by wages from two jobs? If so, when would I have time to enjoy the fruits of my labor? These were my deciding factors: money and how to get it.

The only available options did not appeal to me. They could not pay me enough to live up to the standard of living that I had learned from TV, which is considered appropriate for worthwhile people.

Eventually, I did have two children, but they were not the first conceived. I have talked with my friends, and I am not alone in my concerns. Everyone considers the money factor to be of primary importance. In the current system, love is not affordable. In the NPCB, love would be fully fundable.

A *nonprofit central bank* can remove this consideration—remove the money factor from the decision. The bank can fund whatever is necessary, so the baby can pay for itself, if the birth certificate bond (7) is redirected. The baby can arrive complete with rent, furniture, diapers, and health care supplied weekly at no additional expense to the parents.

Is that too easy? Then how about this: a new baby is awarded $100,000 through a bond and can be distributed at parental discretion. So if the family already has enough money to provide for the child, they can save or invest it. If they want to use it, they can in any way they choose. They can pay off debts, rent, and bills; buy food and clothes; and improve housing or whatever the parents need to use the money for so they can welcome the new bundle of joy.

Removing the money factor from the decision of weather to have a baby is a huge relief, but how about removing it entirely from the family factor? How many hearts have been broken by the money factor?

Affairs of the heart should stay affairs of the heart, and the size of one's wallet should have nothing to do with it. Time and again, I have seen it and felt it, that sense that this person is the right one for me, that we could be so happy together, but I don't make enough money for her parents' approval, or she is from a poorer family. Again, this is the status of the whole world, the *huge* problem of caste systems and classes of society. The NPCB solves it, eliminates it for everyone.

How many bad relationships end in divorce because the money was right but the hearts were wrong? Millions! So if family is important to you, then a *nonprofit central bank* is the way to go. You will be free to live and love as your heart desires.

# Justice

With the predicted reduction in crime, a complement of full-time police officers is not needed. And given the increase in police sadism and brutality on behalf of the for-profit banks, I am not sure they are wanted.

Rather than a large full-time police force, a standing reserve force of peace officers could do the job safer and better than a standing police corps.

The paramilitary aspect of law enforcement could be traded for a more compassionate civil response than the Taser, stick, spray, fist, boot, and gun brand of vigilantism law enforcement epidemic we have today.

Administrators of justice would become immune to bribery and could dedicate themselves to the higher idealistic practice of justice administration.

In the labor-as-money system, the police officers' role in society would be shouldered by every person willing to step in when the time comes. They would receive additional education credits for the training and a monthly bonus in return for obligation to serve should the need arise. They could pay themselves to go to court and follow through on their investigations.

The only full-time police needed would be trainers, detectives, and administrators.

The labor of perfecting and practicing law as a lawyer, judge, and clerk would generate their own desired pay to present disputes in court.

No longer would deep pocketed litigants hold the advantage by driving the price of justice beyond reach. Everyone in justice would be armored against bribery and corruption and be free to serve the highest ideals of justice and ethics.

# Poverty

*Poverty kills more people than all crimes and wars combined.* Poverty supplies the soldiers for the ugly wars raging across the globe. If they have no opportunity, no desire, and no motivation because they are painted into a corner financially and economically disadvantaged, then the escape and pay a stint in the military provides are appealing. They participate for the false belief they will somehow be better off if they win. Win or loose, nothing will change for them; this is the sad truth, and after the physical, mental and emotional stress of war, they are often ruined as a person and some turn to suicide anyway.

An oath of nonviolence will get you an *nonprofit central bank* account anywhere on the globe. Instant funding is available based on the individual's willingness to work.

People will not need to rely on any government, church, or council to have their needs met. If they need food, they can get it; infrastructure can be built, poaching eradicated, and education for all provided.

## Immigration

Right now, there are literally millions of displaced people trying to find a peaceful home. They had a perfectly good home where they were and have been forced to relocate by escalating violence or economic disadvantage. They risk their lives to travel by any means necessary to somewhere there is no warfare or economic hardship, where they can earn some money to send home.

If they had the ability to create money where they were, they would not have to move. Currency unites all races, religions, nationalities. If everyone on both sides of a conflict could be united under a *nonprofit central bank* or the country that creates it, then they would both be on the same side and would have a strong reason to maintain peace and cooperation despite personal and cultural differences.

Should the *nonprofit central bank* become necessarily a bank of this country or that and citizenship are required to receive funds, then it should be so easy to become a financial citizen of that country that travel to, and residence of that home country would not be necessary. That country could take over the world via mass voluntary participation.

## Prostitution and Pornography

The world's oldest profession will still be around. There will no longer be a need for money motivating such potentially self-destructive behavior. No one will have to have sex for money anymore. The only ones doing it will be the ones who want to do it for no other reason than they like it, and that's okay.

## New Industrial Sectors

Accumulating industrial toxic waste is a danger to the whole world. A *nonprofit central bank* can fund the cleanup of the environment. It can fund research, development, deployment, and implementation of industrial-waste containment, collection, processing, and disposal. It can fund new technologies to integrate with industrial manufacture to mitigate industrial toxic waste.

Industrial waste was never profitable, until now. Imagine all the unrecyclable waste being fed into a volcano. Volcanoes are the world's best place for waste disposal, but the money to develop the technology and the logistics involved to transport all the trash to a stable active volcanic site makes it impossible in the current debt-as-money system. Instead they appear to just dump it all in the ocean (39). A labor-as-money system will fund all of it at a profit. *There is plenty of work to be done; this system makes it all possible.*

## Free and Fair Marketplace

A *nonprofit central bank* can provide funding to foster competition. It can provide start-up costs and training to create companies to compete with existing monopolies.

The labor of consumption is the activity of selling or buying. In this system, your work for the day may be to go shopping for groceries.

The nonprofit central bank can create a new class of global citizens. *The consumer class* would use, alone or in combination, the basic income and labor compensation of the NPCB to bridge any gaps and pay off all debts. This creates a permanent-consumption environment and perpetual-profit potential for manufacturers and merchants.

Additionally, a global consumer could have funds created based on the amount of consumption of previous financial quarters. The more you spend, the more you will be able to spend. This can be expanded and can facilitate global free trade.

## Starvation

With labor-created money from the *nonprofit central bank*, homelessness would evaporate. Everyone would have a place to live. If everyone has a place to live, then they have a place to grow some food.

There would no longer be a need to pack into dense city environments, and people could spread out over larger areas of the globe. There they could pay themselves to grow their own food and distribute it. Others would pay themselves for the labor of distributing food.

With food production decentralized, more areas would be available to plant and grow food. In places where the climate is not hospitable to traditional gardening or farming, they can build large vertical hydroponic structures and pay themselves to do it all debt-free.

All this work would be made easier by more hands available and willing to do it as well as automation reducing the labor required. Where food is unavailable, it can now be delivered as well as new facilities created to serve remote areas.

Instead of donating that dollar to feed that child, you could make dollars by feeding those children.

## War

In order to redirect the economic focus of the global economies from destruction to production, military service should disqualify the individual from participation for the duration of their military service. This is not to discriminate against soldiers; rather, it is to encourage peaceful living. There cannot be a war if no one shows up!

The present debt-as-currency system creates unlimited funds with debt, the bulk of which are used to build, support, and encourage numerous wars around the world. The *nonprofit central bank* issuing debt-free funds to hard workers creates an opportunity counterbalance. The potentially unlimited debt-free money one could earn by following their bliss can make the low-wage, dangerous life of suffering that is military service seem foolish and idiotic by comparison.

I am a veteran and am very proud of my military service. It is an honorable profession that provides great personal development. The NPCB system is better because it provides the same opportunity for personal development without the negative, destructive aspects of military service.

The solution is for the individual to claim ownership of his or her labor.

The general populace must create valid, debt-free currency from their labor. A *nonprofit central bank* can facilitate and administrate this activity. The individual can self-issue a bond on all future labor to the *nonprofit central bank*, using the same logic and ideology that validates the fractional reserve banking system. The NPCB can use these bonds as a basis to issue money debt-free. The debt-free currency created will gradually overtake the debt limits and stabilize the world's economies.

The value of gold is an agreement; the value of labor will also be an agreement.

Getting a job requires permission from the employer.

Labor is as good as gold and makes everyone everywhere instantly self-employed and as valuable to the bank as $2 million (or whatever agreed upon) in gold in this system.

They will tell you in school that this is the only system we can have. I cannot imagine how anything so flawed can be irreplaceable. It is obvious that creating money with debt favors the lender. It is not a valid system if the lender creates the currency from nothing. It is much better and more reasonable to create currency from its original source—labor.

In brief, a *nonprofit central bank* orchestrating a labor-generated debt-free money supply is not the cure for all ills. It will not solve every problem in every life, but it will remedy most of the suffering caused by corrupt for-profit banks, like wars, starvation, pollution, and poverty.

It may take one hundred years for these ideas to sink in. I sure hope it doesn't. If it does, the world may not be recognizable. But these ideas could bring it back and may be the only way to fund the resurrection of our world.

# Appendix

## Global Nonprofit Bank Guidelines

The individual must participate voluntarily in the free-money system. By participation, the individual promises to never use violence against another person or cause wanton destruction of private property or the natural environment or allow such violence and destruction, through action or inaction, to occur. The individual promises to never use the funds to support armed conflict of any size. The individual promises to never use the funds to destroy the natural environment for any reason. The individual agrees to receive private sector funds for personal and private use and eligibility for other sector funding as desired. The individual agrees to recognize all other free-money system participants as free people and compatriots before any political, ethnic, religious, or sexual division. The individual agrees to recognize the inalienable rights of others, including but not limited to the Bill of Rights of the US Constitution.

## Private Sector

Private sector basic allowances shall be made available to eligible individual participants on a scheduled basis (see table 1). The individual can decide how often the funds are disbursed—e.g., daily, weekly, or monthly.

Requirements for eligibility are ideally

- a criminal history free of violent crimes for a period of two years;

- no employment or current association with any branch of military, police, or intelligence service for a period of two years;
- commencement of employment with military, police, or intelligence or commission of a violent crime will be grounds for immediate disqualification and cessation of benefits without warning or notification.

Labor-created funds can be distributed to eligible individuals for activities performed by the individual on an hourly basis at an honest and fair rate determined by the participant[5] (table 1). The purpose of this is to enable every individual to be prosperously self-employed first and a subservient worker second. These funds can be collected along with regular pay from all eligible types of work except those that will disqualify the individual mentioned above.

These funds can be adjusted at will by the participant and are intended for but not limited to

- filling the gaps of low wages paid by traditional employers and high costs of living;
- replacing wages paid by employers in times of abrupt unemployment and creating jobs in beneficial but otherwise unprofitable fields like environmental stewardship, endangered-species preservation, area beautification, and recycling efforts;
- compensating the labor of service.

The individual can start an account with the NPCB, which originates a labor bond. This bond should be the equivalent of generous full-time labor for blocks of time. (In my examples, I used twenty-five years and forty dollars per hour.)

The individual then fulfills the bond pledge one hour at a time by doing the labor of choice and logging the time. The individual

---

[5] Ideally, everyone should set their own value of labor. I think a relatively generous standard is a good baseline.

then notifies the NPBC of the time spent working and is immediately compensated by creation of fresh-money deposit in the account.

Once the individual has fulfilled 10 percent of the bond's value, the bond is vested, and two things happen:

- The individual is awarded an open credit limit not to exceed 80 percent of the average labor-earned balance.
- The bond is grouped with other vested bonds by the NPCB into mutual funds that will be used as securities for grants and credits in the public sector not to exceed 90 percent of the fund totals.

## Public Sector

Public sector funds can be generated debt-free to serve the communities, including but not limited to development and maintenance of infrastructure, public transportation, coordination of city planning, code enforcement, zoning, regulation, and oversight of business/industry/education facility design, construction, and maintenance (table 4).

The Government Coordination Office or equivalent would be the hub of public works and services.

Business/industrial sector funds can be distributed to eligible sole proprietors upon approval of the coordinating authority for new business and, by request, for participation of existing business (table 5). By participation, the business agrees to enjoy guaranteed profits of no less than 20 percent and no more than 500 percent.

Public business / industrial sector funds will be available to build new facilities in coordination with city planners, environmental considerations, market sharing, and institutionalized competition to eliminate monopolies in every sector and develop new sectors with regard to environmental sustainability (table 6).

These funds shall also be made available to develop and implement merchandise tracking. The purpose of this is to track the longevity of use of durable goods so as to pay residual bonuses to manufacturers and laborers who physically constructed the goods (table

7). They will make the data (such as failures, repair histories, and successes) available to manufactures and consumers in order to foster improved design and materials for greater longevity of use.

Education sector funds can be distributed to eligible individuals for every unit of study completed with high marks from high school onward (table3). For those individuals who so desire to serve the community at large, they may study emergency medicine, administration of justice, firefighting, and social sciences. Upon earning a certificate, singularly or by combination, the individual contracts to use their knowledge and expertise should the need arise; they can collect additional funds.

Public sector funds can be paid out to first responders receiving additional education funds and to implement and supervise licensure requirements and response protocols through the Government Coordination Office.

These funds are intended to offset the cost of kit required to competently perform the social service (e.g., medical personnel should have a medical treatment bag stocked and handy). Should the individual encounter a situation and not respond, after a peer review, they would be disqualified from receiving the additional funds.

Public sector funds can be used to encourage participation and optimistic public attitudes in print and media. Media programming subsidized by public sector funds must have an overall message of tolerance, education, cooperation, and nonviolence, and the services and products funded by the nonprofit central bank can be advertised at a discount rate.

Eligible public sector construction projects should have 110 percent of their power needs supplied by solar, wind, and other renewable sources (table 6). The structures should be resistant to earthquakes, severe weather, tornados and hurricanes, fire, mold, and flooding. They should be constructed out of readily available, easily renewable material of low environmental impact.

Health care sector funds can be paid to licensed health care providers for services rendered on a case-by-case basis (table 1). Health care funds can pay for all allied health professionals to raise current wages to desirable levels, attract more personnel to underserved areas, foster overall improved health care.

*Public sector mutual funds are the foundation of credit issued for individual basic allowance and all other public sector endeavors.*

## Basic Allowance

Basic allowance is an open public credit system that provides debt-free funds to the individual based on consumer spending. The initial basic allowance for eligible individuals is the government-established poverty level cost of living. Thereafter, the limit is raised by totaling the previous two months' spending. If the subsequent month is less than the total limit, the limit remains unchanged.

Basic allowance eligibility is a labor account. With every transaction, the consumer, the merchant or the service provider, and the bank itself originate new money as transaction credits. The balance of transaction credits in the consumer accounts system will supply the basis for first-line credit to cover the individual basic allowance. The secondary credit line is the bank's transaction account, and the tertiary line is the body of labor bond mutual funds.

Labor makes money, service makes money, and consumption makes money.

The money created as compensation for labor is the real money foundation to be regarded as gold in the vault. The bonds are issued individually and organized collectively by the *nonprofit central bank* as securities, like mutual funds. These will be the basis for creation of credit currency for public sector subsidies as needed. Public sector subsidies like business stabilization (table 5) and other services are beneficial but not otherwise profitable, like health care, education, infrastructure environmental stewardship, recycling . . .

## The Consumer Class

The consumer class operates independently of labor but interacts with the public and private sectors. The mutual bond securities will be the final safety net. An individual free of a history of violent crime for two years and not currently engaged in any military, police, or intelligence service would be eligible for a basic consumer allowance of debt-free currency for use with regard to activities of local consumption of goods and services offered. This initial sum will be granted in the equivalent amount of US$2,500. For every transaction completed in the system, a transaction credit will be generated for the consumer, supplier, and bank. The consumer credit will look like a cash-back reward. The supplier credit will look like a 20 percent subsidy of gross receipts. The bank credit will look like a deposit in the general fund supporting all consumption. These amounts will be created with the labor associated with consumption.

For the consumer, if a consumer spends more than the $2,500 a month, the limit is raised by adding the previous two months' expenditures. If the previous month's expenditures do not exceed the limit, the limit remains unchanged.

For the public supplier, a global reduction of price of 10 percent is required to participate in the system. All of the gross receipts are totaled and are subsidized to at least 20 percent. Operating expenses are subsidized at reasonable rates, and quarterly profits beyond 500 percent are returned to the bank fund as new deposits.

Tables 1 and 2

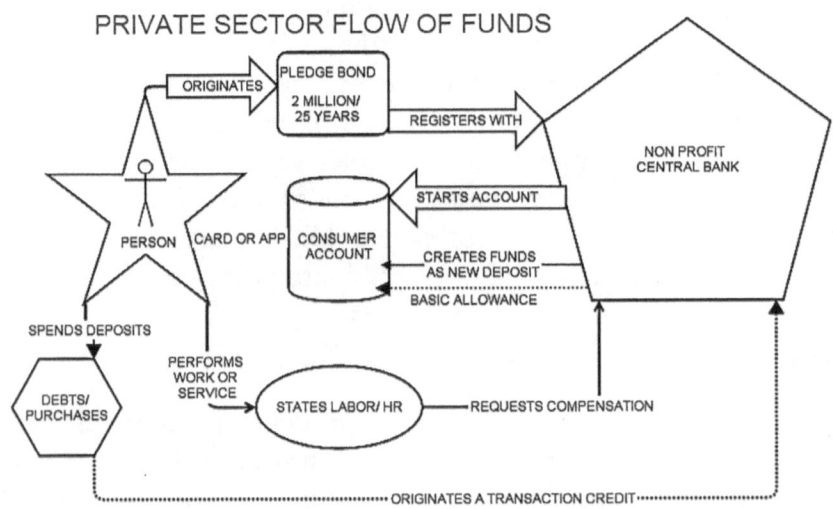

# A CURE FOR SLAVERY

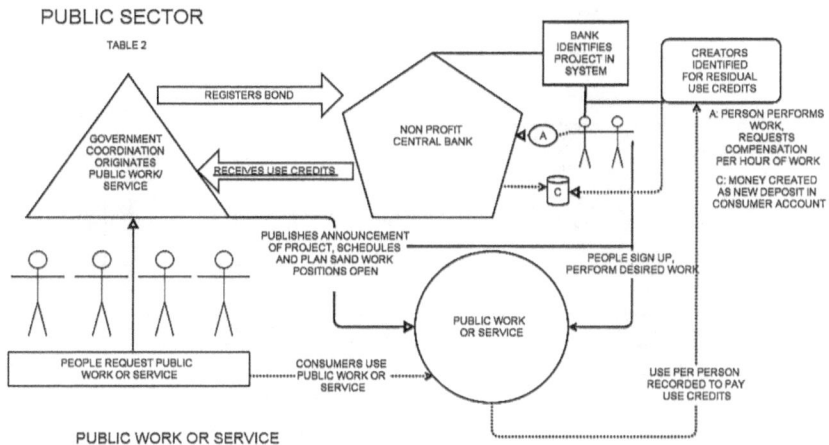

Table 3

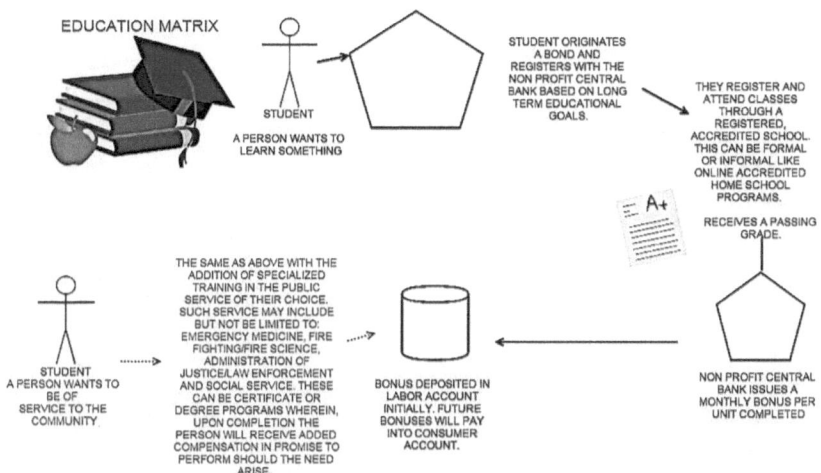

## Table 4. Public Sector

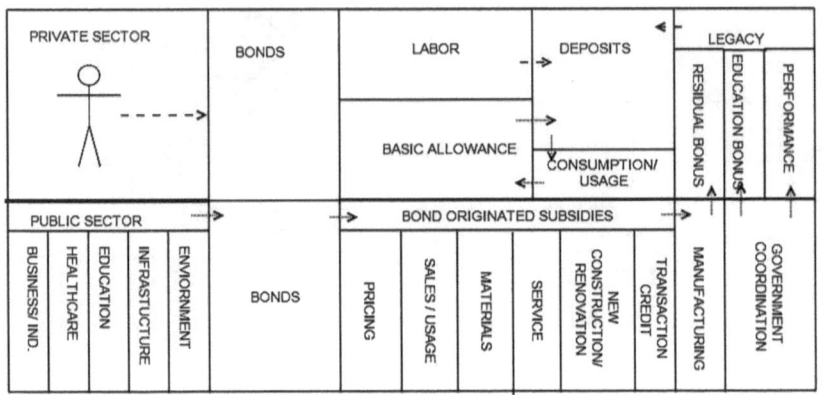

## Table 5

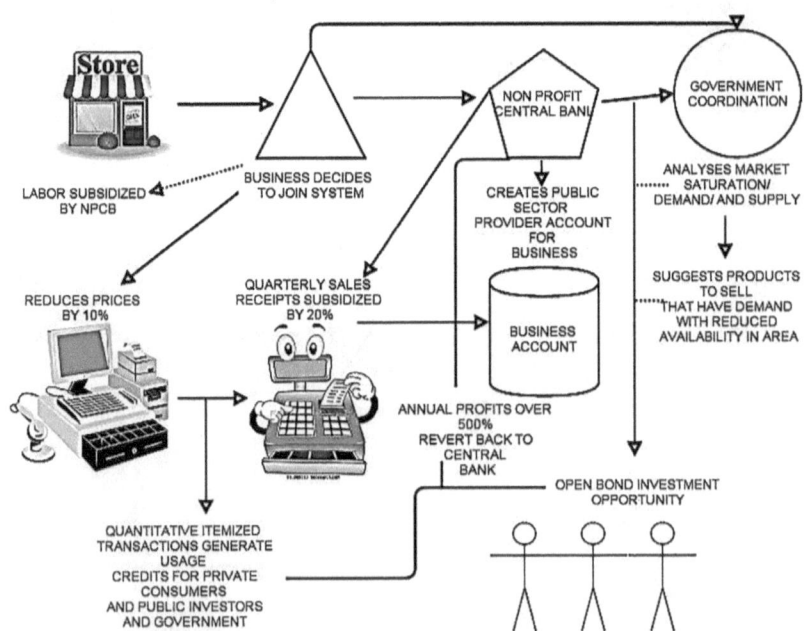

# A CURE FOR SLAVERY

## Table 6

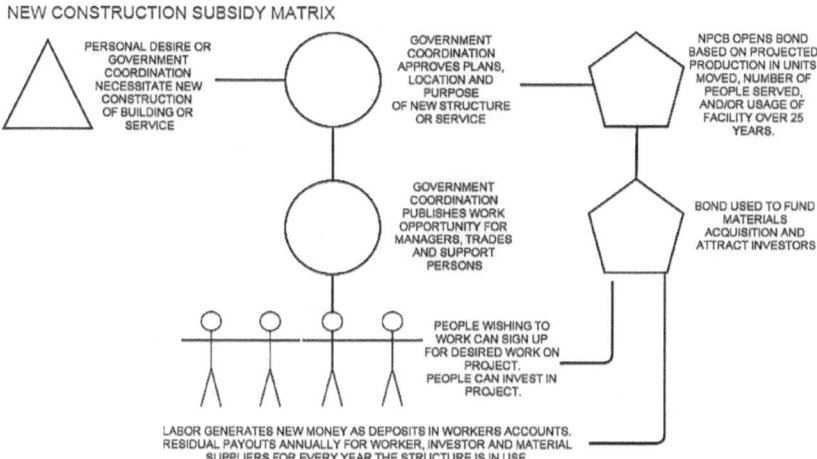

## Table 7

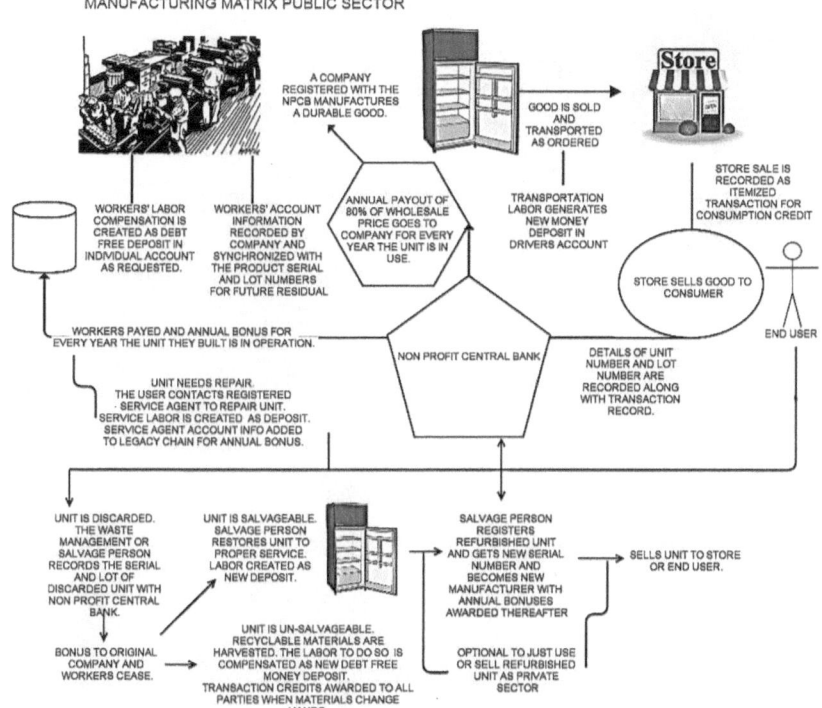

## Table 7A

MANUFACTURING MATRIX PRIVATE SECTOR

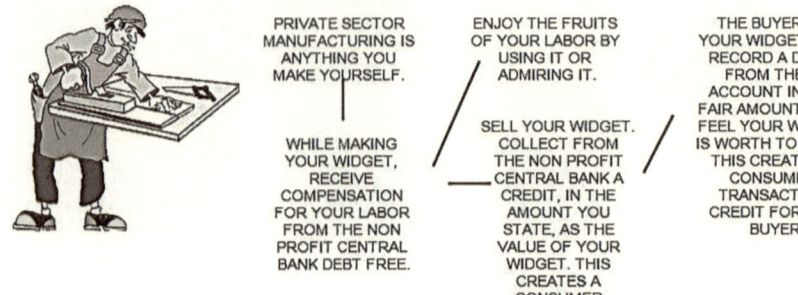

## Table 8

INFRASTRUCTURE MATRIX

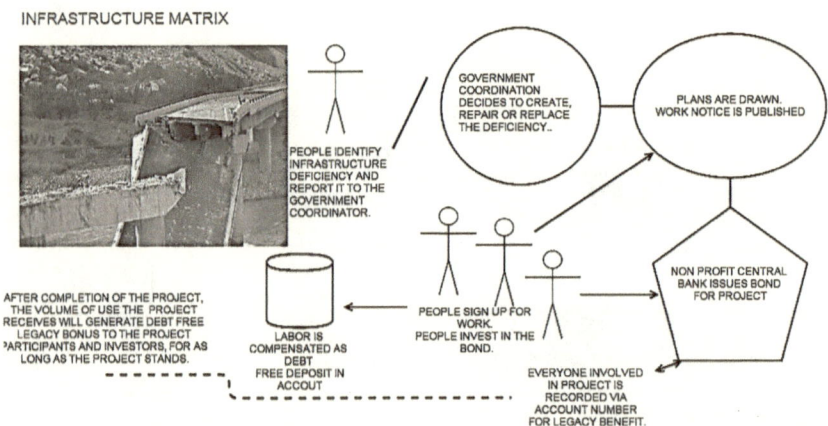

# Table 9

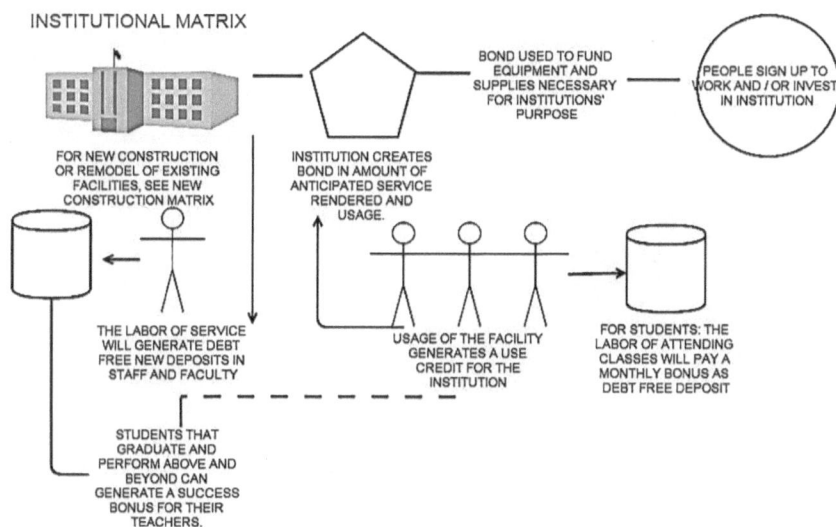

## Hospitals

Two bonds would be required—one for initial construction and a second for service based on anticipated usage. As the patients come in for treatment, they would sign in as usual. This record could be redeemed for usage credits from the NPCB. Additionally, the patients can invest in the usage bonds and become stockholders.

## Schools and Universities

Schools and universities could be structured as above with the addition that students could come with bonds based on educational goals. These bonds could be used as a basis to credit the institution for daily usage for attendance and participation as well as credit the student for completed units.

# Bibliography

1. Hanson, Jay, "From capitalism to democracy: From complexity to simplicity," last modified July 10, 2012, accessed September 10, 2015, www.dieoff.org, www.jayhanson.org/oldindex.htm.
2. Maloney, Mike, "Biggest Scam in the History of Mankind," *Hidden Secrets of Money*, episode 4, 2014.
3. Russo, Alan. *America: Freedom to Fascism*, 2006.
4. "The panic of 1907," www.thegoldstandardnow.org/the-panic-of-1907.
5. "Federal Reserve Act," December 23, 1913, https://fraser.stlouisfed.org/.
6. Griffin, G. Edward, *The Creature from Jekyll Island: A Second Look at the Federal Reserve*, 1998, ISBN: 13: 978-0912986326.
7. Kelly, Patrick, *Meet Your Strawman*, August 20, 2015, www.yourstrawman.com/strawman.pdf.
8. Improve Your Score, www.myfico.com/crediteducation/improveyourscore.aspx.
9. Maloney, Mike, *The Case for $20,000 Oz Gold: Debt Collapse*, 2011.
10. Locke, John, *The Second Treatise of Civil Government*, 6th s.l.: Ebooks@adelaide, 1690, 6th edition, 1764.
11. Smith, Adam, *An Inquiry into the Nature and Causes of the Wealth of Nations*, London: W. Strahan and T. Cadell, 1776.

12. Curtis, Adam, *The Century of the Self*, BBC documentary series, BBC, 2002.
13. "I, King Edward," Edict of Expulsion, 1290.
14. Maslow, Abraham. *A theory of human motivation*, 1943.
15. Curtis, Adam. *The Century of the Self*, BBC documentary series, 2002.
16. Debt.org/credit/loans/, www.debt.org. This site gives terrible advice on the use of credit cards.
17. Jacobs, Andrew, "Behind a Plea for Help from a China Labor Camp: Halloween Decorations Sold in US Hid a Letter Calling Attention to Abuse," *International Herald Tribune*, June 13, 2013.
18. Schecter, Danny, *Plunder: The Crime of Our Time*, 2009.
19. Smith, Edward H., *Confessions of a Confidence Man: A Handbook for Suckers*, New York: Scientific American Publishing Company, 1923, pp. 35–37.
20. Melendez, Eleazar David, "US Overdraft Fees Jump to 32 billion as New Rules Prove Ineffective," *Huffington Post Business*, March 29, 2013.
21. Greenwald, Robert, *Walmart: The High Cost of Low Price*, 2005.
22. Pereau, Ross, Ross Preau: US Presidential Debate, 1992, 1992, https://www.youtube.com/watch?v=Jg9qB_BIjWY.
23. Fox, Louis, *Story of Stuff*, Funders Workgroup for Sustainable Production and Consumption, 2007.
24. The Amazing ROI of Corporate Lobbying, s.l.: United Republic, July 03, 2012.
25. *The Men Who Built America*, History Channel, 2012.
26. GcMAF.se, accessed September 16, 2015, https://gcmaf.se.
27. Mercola, Joseph. Vaccines and Neurological Damage. Mercola Take Control of Your Health. http://www.mercola.com/article/vaccines/neurological_damage.htm.

28. Chase Manhattan's Emerging Markets Group Memo, New York: Internal Memo Chase Manhattan Bank, 1995. Internal Memo. Memo from bank to Mexican consulate regarding civil war in Southern state of Chiapas and investor confidence . ... .

http://www.realhistoryarchives.com/collections/hidden/chase-memo.htm

29. Wilson, Brian, *The Slippery Slope: US Military Moves into Mexico*, 1998.

30. McLaughlin, Martin, "Clinton, Republicans Agree to Deregulation of US Financial System," November 1, 1999.

31. The Stanford Prison Experiment, s.l. : Psychology Department Stanford University, 1971.

32. Grace, Peter, Grace Commission Report, New York: Macmillan Publishing Company, 1984. The president's private sector survey on cost control.

33. Roosevelt, Franklin D., the New Deal, a series of domestic programs enacted in the United States between 1933 and 1938.

34. Maloney, Mike. *The Hidden Secrets of Money*, episode 1. 2011.

35. Nobel, Scott. "The Deep State," *Counter-Intelligence*, Metonia, 2013.

36. Kranzler, Dave, "The Latest Heist: US Quietly Snatches the Ukraine's Gold Reserves," 21stcenturywire.com, March 21, 2014, http://21stcenturywire.com/2014/03/21/the-latest-heist-us-quietly-snatches-the-ukrainian-gold-reserves/.

37. "Man invents machine to convert plastic into oil," United Nations University, 2010.

38. *What did we learn from click frenzy?* Blog, Woolworths@carat.blogger.com, 2012, http://dailyintelligenceupdate.blogspot.com.

39. Milman, Oliver. Full-Scale of Plastic in the World's Oceans Revealed for First Time. *The Guardian*, Pollution, 2014, US edition.

# About the Author

Mr. Parker was born and lives in the United States. His great grandparents on his father's side were actual slaves on a cotton plantation in Oklahoma. He lived in Greece as a child on the island of Crete and, most recently, in Russia in the city of Novosibirsk.

Mr. Parker's background includes almost twenty years of clinical patient care as a back-office medical assistant and is now a world-class massage therapist.

He had a real estate license from 2004 to 2008 and saw firsthand the corruption and destruction of the real estate bubble and crash.

Mr. Parker has been described as smarter than the average bear and a smart-ass with a gift for problem-solving. He has applied his gift in this text in order to solve what "experts" appear to regard as unsolvable problems related to economic sociology.

www.ingramcontent.com/pod-product-compliance
Lightning Source LLC
Chambersburg PA
CBHW030741180526
45163CB00003B/878